The Ultimate Guide to Text and Phone Game

Version 1.0

by Braddock & Mr. M

The Ultimate Guide to Text and Phone Game
Version 1.0

by Braddock co-written and edited by Mr. M

Copyright 2010, 2011, 2012 Love Systems, Inc. All Rights Reserved

Published by:

Classic Books Publishing
Dr. Christoph Lymbersky
Luetkensallee 41
22041 Hamburg
Germany

Classic Books Publishing is a label of the MLP Management Laboratory Press UG, registered in Hamburg, Germany.

Disclaimer:

All rights reserved. No part of this publication may be reproduced or distributed in any form or by any means, or stored in a database or retrieval system, without the prior written consent of Love Systems Inc., including but not limited to, in any network or other electronic storage or transmission, or broadcast for distance learning. This work is not to be considered professional, medical, psychological or legal advice. It is for entertainment purposes only. Love Systems, Inc., or our associates, or affiliates will not be liable for any direct or indirect consequences that occur from the use of any of the ideas contained this book.

Publication date: June 2012, Hamburg, Germany

Registered with: ISBN-Agentur für die Bundesrepublik Deutschland in der MVB Marketing- und Verlagservice des Buchhandels GmbH Bibliografische Information der Deutschen Nationalbibliothek: Die Deutsche Nationalbibliothek verzeichnet diese Publikation in der Deutschen Nationalbibliografie; detaillierte bibliografische Daten sind im Internet über http://dnb.d-nb.de abrufbar.

Front Cover Picture: © Classic Books Publishing & Love Systems Inc.
Interior Pictures: : © Love Systems Inc.
Text Layout: : © Classic Books Publishing

When ordering this title, use **ISBN: 978 3 941579 72 9**

Contents

A Note from the Author	11
Acknowledgments	13
Introduction	15
Chapter 1 – Turning Her Phone Number into a Date	**21**
The Aims (Goals) of Text and Phone Game	23
The Basics of Turning a Phone Number into a Date	24
Running Solid Game	24
Time Bridging	25
Solidifying the Connection	28
Peer Group Approval	29
Set Frames of Expectation and Congruence	29
Asking For the Phone Number	30
Make Sure that She has Your Phone Number	30
Text Her While She's Standing In Front Of You	31
Chapter 2 - Basic Concepts in Text and Phone Game	**37**
Callback Humor	37
Using Callback Humor in Voicemail	38
Using Callback Humor in Text Messaging	38
Seeding Callback Humor during the Initial Interaction	39
Avoid Overusing Callback Humor on the Same Topic	40
Developing Your Callback Humor Muscles	41
Callback Humor Example	42
Callback Humor Exercise	43
Investment Building	45
Examples of High and Low Investment	46
Chapter 3 – First Contact	**53**
Considering her Investment Levels	54
The "Yes's" and "No's" Law of Investment	54
Boiling a Frog	55
An Example of How the Phone Call can be a Problem	57
Sending the First Text	59
Texting Her Quickly	59
What to Say in the First Text	60
3 Common Mistakes to Avoid in the First Text	62

Early Text and Phone Game – After the Initial Reply	65
The Crucial Question	65
A Summary of the Rules for Early Text Messaging	65
The Structure of Good Text Messaging	69
Early Comfort Building Text Messages	73
Cycling Push/Pull: Building Comfort While Maintaining Attraction	74
Early Comfort Pitfalls to Avoid	77
Examples of Early Comfort Texts	79
Increase the Frequency and Intensity of Communication	81
Going for the Meet Up	81
Baiting for Low Investment Situations	82
Introduction - Explaining Dynamite Theory	89
Short Fuses	90
Short Fuses Defined	90
How to Recognize a Short Fuse	90
What Can Cause A Short Fuse?	91
Signs and Symptoms of a Short Fuse	91
Examples of Short Fuses	92
Medium Fuses	98
Medium Fuse Defined	98
How to Recognize a Medium Fuse	98
What Can Cause a Medium Fuse?	98
Signs and Symptoms of a Medium Fuse	99
Examples of Medium Fuses	100
Long Fuses	106
Long Fuses Defined	106
How to Recognize a Long Fuse	107
What Can Cause a Long Fuse?	107
What Can Cause A Long Fuse?	108
Signs and Symptoms of a Long Fuse	109
Examples of Long Fuses	110
Chapter 5 -Strategies for Each Fuse	**125**
Go for the Date	125
No Need to Spend Too Much Time on the Phone With a Short Fuse	126
Do Not Over Text: Avoid Making a Short Fuse Long	128
Medium Fuse Strategies	133

Extending a "You Guys Should Meet Us Out" Invite	134
Burn Her Down to a Short Fuse	135
Long Fuse Strategies	139
Pinging and Keeping on Her Radar	139
A Covert Tactic - the Mass Text	140
Do Not Seem Too Excited	141
Do Not Get Emotional	141
Have a Number of Long Fuses in Play	142
Be Patiently Persistent	143
Chapter 6 – Further Text and Phone Game Tactics	**153**
The Ideal Days to Text	153
The Ideal Time to Text	153
Pinging	154
Baiting	156
Playing Roles	157
Messages For Short or Medium Fuses on Pause	159
Pull Back On The Reins (Correcting Bad Behavior)	160
Voicemail	162
Chapter 7 - Building Value and Generating Attraction	**167**
Told Versus Observed	167
Examples of Texts for Each Attraction Trigger	168
Health	168
Social Intuition	169
Humor	170
Status and Wealth	173
Confidence	174
Pre-selection	175
Challenge	176
Tempo	176
What Is Tempo?	176
Manipulating Tempo – Using The Law of Varying	176
Returns	176
Frame Setting	178
Getting Her to Take Positive Action	179
More Text Message Attraction Strategies	181

Examples of Attraction Generating Text Message Exchanges	181
Qualification over Text Message	189

Chapter 8 - Sexualization — 195

The Pro's and Con's of Sexualization	196
'Player'	196
'Creep'	197
'Horny 7th Grader'	197
Proper Sexualization	198
The Key Concepts of Sexualization	199
50:50 Power Ratio or Better	199
Power Ratio and Fuse Length	200
Baiting and Mirroring Her Sexual Intent	201
Sexual Hoops for Text and Phone Game	203
Sexual Hoops: Stage 1	203
Sexual Hoops: Stage 2	205
Sexual Sexual Hoops: Stage 3	207
Sexual Hoops: Stage 4	213
Important Notes on Sexual Hoops	217
Sexual Hoops Summary	218
False Barriers	218
How to use False Barriers	219
Real False Barriers	220
Booty Call Phone and Texting	222
Friends With Benefits: Putting it All Together:	226
How To Text Friends With Benefits: The Art Of The Booty Call Text	229
Sexualization on the Phone	230

Chapter 9 - Meet Up Strategies — 237

A Few Common Mistakes	237
Avoid Making the Meet up a Formal Process	237
Suggest a Meet Up at a High Point in the Conversation	237
Do Not 'Over Game'	238
The Basic Structure of Going for the Meet Up	238
Example of a Bad Phone Call:	242
Example of a Good Phone Call:	243
The Distracter Technique (credit DaHunter)	245

Meet Up Strategies Based on Fuse Length	247
Short Fuse	247
Medium and Long Fuses	247

Chapter 10 - Situations and Scenarios — 253

What to do if investment is very low?	254
What to do if investment is very high?	256
What if she is sending mixed signals? i.e. 'She flirts but I don't know where I stand!'	257
What to do if it was on, but it's gone cold: texting to get back in the game!	258
What to text?	258
What happens if you did not get far into the initial interaction but you get on the phone with her somehow?	261
Other Scenarios	262
Texting girls in other cities or far away	262
Social circle text game	263

Chapter 11 - Revitalizing Old Numbers — 269

What to text?	269

Chapter 12 - Flaking — 277

What should you do if a woman flakes?	280
Closing Remarks	282
Further Education	283
FREE Resources to Improve Your Game	285
Terms and Conditions	286
Contributors To This Book	287

A Note from the Author

Thank you for purchasing The Ultimate Guide to Text and Phone Game. This book was designed to give you a road map to follow in your text messages and telephone interactions with women.

There are literally an infinite number of styles, angles, and outcomes that are possible when using text messages and phone calls and no one product could describe all situations that can and will appear. Nonetheless, we have taken cutting edge techniques and concepts and distilled them into one book. Within these pages are the field tested, proven theories and methods that have helped us convert phone numbers into dates with high consistency.

Use this book as a road map to help you hit waypoints, but not as a set of rigid rules that you feel must follow religiously.

Human interactions are as much an art as they are a science. As such, it is crucial that you take this technology and add your own individuality and flavor to it. Remember that the objective is not to replace your personality, but to give you a deep understanding of the psychology, techniques, and principles behind text and phone interactions.

The best in any field are those who can determine when to respect a rule and when to break it. As you get better at internalizing and incorporating the principles in this book, you will notice that there are nuances in the use of the rules outlined, including occasionally breaking those rules.

The Ultimate Guide to Phone and Text Game assumes a base level understanding of the Emotional Progression Model found in Magic Bullets.

Writing this book has been an endeavor of passion and dedication to me. Within it is encoded a system, a system learned the 'hard way' – through trial and error, hard work, difficult situations, tears and triumphs. It has literally taken me (and the various others who have contributed to the making of this book) years to discover what you now have in front of you. It's my hope that by utilizing concepts in The Ultimate Guide to Phone and Text Game, you get a new understanding of how to better use your texts and calls to get more dates.

So thanks again for purchasing The Ultimate Guide to Text and Phone Game. I hope it helps you to achieve the success that you are looking for, with the wonderful women that you desire.

- **Braddock**, Senior Love Systems Instructor, January 2010

Acknowledgments

When I first sat down to write this book, I thought it would be a breeze. After about 200 pages of writing and a year of frustration, I finally decided to ask my close friend and mentor Mr M to take a look at it. I expected a quick read and a few edits.
It was not to be. We ended up diving into this thing; logging countless hours, changing the content, arguing over principles, discussing, sharing, and laughing at old drafts. If Mr M hadn't decided to take such an active role in the creation of this book, you would not be reading it right now. I can't thank him enough for the organization and for his painstaking labor in editing and refining drafts. He is as responsible for the completion of this book as I am.

I would also like to thank my good friend Larry P for his contributions and game insight. You are truly a natural.

I would like to thank Jim, Mark W, and London Wizard, and Sara K for helping with the editing phase of this book.

I would also like to think Aaron Wolverton for all the graphic design associated with this book. You guys were a huge help and did a great job.

Introduction

How do Text and Phone Game fit into Love Systems?

Learning Love Systems can be compared to learning golf. To be a truly great golfer, a player must have the ability to hit with every club in his bag. He must be as good with his driver as he is with his sand wedge.

Love Systems works the same way.. To be decent or better than your 'average man', a guy only needs to have the ability to start a conversation with a woman he doesn't know and get her laughing.

As long as he goes out and does this enough, he should have far better results than the majority of his peers.

However, to enjoy the highest level of success, developing proficiency in the three aspects of the Love Systems Triad Model – Emotional, Physical and Logistical is essential. This means being skilled in approaching, building attraction, qualifying, building comfort, escalating touch, utilizing your text messages, handling the date, escalating sexually, manipulating logistics, and managing a relationship (or multiple relationships). For optimal results, the ability to do all of these in niches such as social circles, day game, same night lays, and strippers and hired guns as necessary.

The key is realizing that increasing your skill even a little, in all of these areas, will greatly increase your overall results. You will also find that

---

A Brief Look at the Love Systems Triad Model

In the **Triad Model** Savoy states:

Most women – especially beautiful women who are used to a lot of attention from men - won't sleep with someone new unless at least three specific factors are present:

- She feels the right kind of emotional connection with you.
- She has a physical connection with you.
- The two of you are alone somewhere where sex can reasonably happen.

The three parts of the breakthrough Love Systems Triad Model are Emotional, Physical, and Logistical. You need to progress each of these three aspects of an interaction in order to go from meeting a woman to successfully entering a sexual relationship with her.

being deficient in any one area will lead to frustration, as you are unable to progress further.

For many people who study and apply Love Systems; Text and Phone Game represents one of the most challenging hurdles to achieving the next level of success. Students consistently report that they have trouble converting phone numbers into dates. The key purpose of Text and Phone Game is to get a woman to meet you again. Some dating products will teach you how to have 'phone sex'. This one does not. The focus of this book is to show you the quickest, most effective way to get to 'real sex' with highly attractive women.

A Personal Account of My Experience of Text and Phone Game by Braddock

I once thought the cell phone was the worst invention ever created. When I had a serious girlfriend, my cell phone was essentially a 'wireless leash' that my girlfriend used to make sure I wasn't having any fun. Invisible handcuff, if you will.

Early on in my journey as a single guy trying to learn Love Systems, I felt like my cell phone was my worst enemy - my kryptonite. After approaching countless women and finally tasting decent success at getting numbers, it was as if the phone was yet another huge roadblock thrown in the path to sex.

I had become confident enough to approach women and ask them for a phone number, but I had zero understanding of what work needed to be done during that first encounter. Often, I found that a number wasn't worth the paper it was written on. For months I would go out and get a bunch of phone numbers, only to have most, if not all,, turn into nothing. It was the same thing every time - I either found myself nervously talking to a girl's voicemail or calling a girl and awkwardly getting off the phone with her minutes later, having murdered any attraction that she once had for me. The problem was that I had NO understanding of what it took to convert a phone number into something tangible, whether this be by phone or text.

It took countless phone numbers, endless awkward conversations, angry hair pulling, and trial and error before I finally began to see the writing on the wall. But once it clicked, I began to see the cell phone as the greatest
discovery since sliced bread. It was as though I had an Uzi in my hands for all these years and only just realized how to turn the safety off!

Soon, I was converting a phone numbers into a date almost every time.

It was blowing my mind how easily numbers, which would have been worthless to me in past were panning out into solid dates. This was holding true with phone numbers pulled from hot girls in five minutes, numbers taken when either I was drunk, or old phone numbers that went 'dead' because of some logistical road block (e.g. maybe she got a boyfriend).

I began to see patterns forming. I noticed that different situations required different tactics. Like any good game, high level Text and Phone Game requires Calibration. The key is to understand how far along you are with the woman. This usually depends on what happened in the initial meeting. Most guys try a 'one size fits all' approach to Text and Phone Game, without understanding that each encounter creates a different terrain and each terrain has a specific vehicle specialized for handling that terrain. You wouldn't drive a Monster Truck on the autobahn and you wouldn't drive a Ferrari on a rocky mountain trail. Having great Text and Phone Game often comes down to choosing which vehicle is best.

CHAPTER 1 – TURNING HER PHONE NUMBER INTO A DATE

IN THIS CHAPTER:

- What it Means to 'Get Her Phone Number'
- The Aims (Goals) of Text and Phone Game
- The Basics of Turning a Phone Number into a Date
- Time Bridging
- Solidifying the Connection
- Peer Group Approval
- Set Frames of Expectation and Congruence
- Asking for the Phone Number
- Text her While She's Standing In Front Of You

THE ULTIMATE GUIDE TO TEXT AND PHONE GAME

Chapter 1 – Turning Her Phone Number into a Date

Changing Your Mindset: What it Means to 'Get Her Phone Number'

Let us set the scene for you. You first meet a woman - whether at a bar, through friends, or on the street - and get into a conversation.

You think that things are going well. You seem to be moving through the Emotional Progression Model and following the Love Systems Triad Model. Somewhere along the line, you make the decision to go for her phone number.

Most men make the assumption that if they did well enough to get a woman's phone number then:

(a) she must like him
(b) a date is a sure thing
(c) sex occurring is likely

However, in most cases this couldn't be further from the truth.
Any guy who has met and dated a lot of women, knows that often times securing a number doesn't mean anything beyond just that. As Nick Savoy sais in Magic Bullets, "A phone number is not a date and vice versa. A phone number is merely a chance at a date."

If you've ever been friends with, or dated an extremely beautiful woman, you probably have a good idea just how many times she gets approached. These women typically say that they do not give their number out 'that often'. This may be true when compared to the amount of times they actually are approached. But even if they only give their phone number to a fraction of these guys, they are still giving their number out fairly frequently.

While women do commonly give out their number to guys they genuinely like, this is not always the case. Some of the more general reasons women give out their numbers include: the feeling of guilt or obligation, pity, validation, or feeling a fleeting moment of attraction. This can be confusing, because why wouldn't she just say "no" if she wasn't into you? Often, she is trying to avoid an uncomfortable confrontation. After being approached countless times, she knows how awkward it can be when a guy reacts poorly to being shot down.

This is a source of great confusion for men. The act of her giving her phone number provides the guy with a false sense of hope and makes him believe that he is further along than he really is.

Once you have spent a fair amount of time approaching women, you will

---

The Emotional Progression Model (EMP)

Below is a brief summary of the EPM. The EPM is the central aspect of the Love Systems Triad Model. See for a full description of the EPM.

Approach
- Start talking to her using field tested openers
- Get off the opener as quickly as possible

Transition
- Start a new thread of conversation
- Lead the conversation and cut threads that are not advantageous

Attraction
- Stimulate her emotionally
- Demonstrate value

Qualification
- Make her work for you
- Find out about her

Comfort
- Find commonalities and build trust
- Show vulnerability and understanding

Seduction
- Avoid state breaks
- Use freeze-outs

Relationship

begin to develop a sense of when a number has promise or when it's likely to turn out as a 'flake'. Developing this sense takes much of the guesswork and emotional sting out of why there was no answer to your call or response to a text message.

It also helps to determine what strategy to use based on how solid or weak a particular phone number is (this is discussed in depth in Chapter 4). No matter how good you get at meeting women, there will always be some component of probability. The goal should never be 'perfection'. There will be times when you run excellent game, text or call at just the right time, and she just doesn't reply.

A flake is when a woman (a) does not reply back to your phone calls or text messages or (b) sets up a meeting and does not show up (or cancels at the last minute).

It's important to realize that you have no idea what is going on in her life. She could have a boyfriend she didn't mention; she could have some weird rule where she only dates guys she meets through friends; she could have lost her phone; she may be extremely busy; you may have typed the wrong number (it only takes a digit); etc. The reasons are endless.

Do not assume that every number that does not work out is a reflection of your 'poor game' or some flaw that she saw in you.

The key is to be ok with that! To get good at Text and Phone Game, you must develop an 'abundance' mind set. Women come and go, and many will flake. Each phone number must be viewed as nothing more than a chance to practice and/or a loose lead. As a friend says, "Women are like buses, if you miss one it's no big deal. Another one will come around in 10 minutes."

The Aims (Goals) of Text and Phone Game

Initially, getting a phone number should be a goal in and of itself. Never forget that it's an achievement for you to even get a woman's phone number. However, while reading and applying the principals of Text and Phone Game, there are three additional goals which you should keep in mind:

1. **Arranging logistics:** In some interactions, you may be able to escalate further than just getting a phone number. An example of this would be if you meet a girl and take her home with you that night. Realize, logistics do not always allow for this (e.g. if she has lots of friends around her, preventing her from going home with you). You

may find yourself in a situation where text and phone is the only alternative for further escalation.

2. **Converting phone numbers into dates:** When you find yourself getting phone numbers consistently, you will need to focus on converting these phone numbers into actual meet ups.

3. **Generating attraction and comfort:** In order to secure an actual meet up, you may need to generate attraction and comfort through text messages and phone conversations.

These three aims will be addressed constantly throughout this book.

The Basics of Turning a Phone Number into a Date

We have established that "a phone number is not a date and vice versa. A phone number is merely a chance at a date."
However, there are still quite a few things that you can and should do when first meeting a woman to solidify your chances of turning a phone number into a date. Following the simple suggestions outlined below can virtually cut your work in half when making your first text or call.

Running Solid Game

One of the most important things that you can do to solidify the phone number is to make sure that you have been running solid game leading up to calling her. Running solid game simply means that you followed the Emotional Progression Model all the way through to the comfort phase. The further you get in the model, the more solid the number will be for you later.

To create a good chance of seeing her again, you need to establish at least some comfort during the first interaction. To get to the comfort phase, you need to first approach, transition, attract, and qualify her. If you only have 10 minutes for this, it simply means that you have to play faster.

Of course, there are times when this is logistically difficult. Always go for the number, even in these circumstances. Just be aware that in these cases, you may have your Text and Phone Game work cut out for you, in regards to converting the number into an actual date.

While it's outside the scope of this book to give an in depth explanation of each phase of the Emotional Progression Model, it is important that you understand the sequence the model follows. If you've never seen this model before, we highly suggest that you read Magic Bullets.

Time Bridging

Most guys make the mistake of asking a woman for her phone number without at least hinting at an actual plan for when and why they should see each other again. In other words, they forget to 'time bridge'. A time bridge is during the initial interaction, when you set up a definite plan to meet at a later date.

In Magic Bullets, Savoy writes, "Focus on the date, not the phone number.

The phone number should be an afterthought..." At some point in the conversation (before taking her phone number and without inviting her), you want to discuss things going on in your life that you plan on doing in the near future.

> **A Caveat: The Benefit of Fast Number Closing**
>
> Although fast number closes often lead to flakes, you should spend at least a few months trying for the phone number of every girl that you approach. By doing this, you will have trained yourself to ask for the phone number without even thinking about it. It will also give you a 'feel' for both **(a)** when you should ask for a number and **(b)** which numbers will flake. You can only develop this 'feel' from approaching and interacting with numerous women.

Future plans do not have to be grandiose, but they should be specific. "We should hang out sometime" is a weak time bridge because it is non-specific. While it does a fair job of keeping things low pressure, her mind does not have to visualize or accept that the two of you will ever actually meet again.

An ideal time bridge and number close will flow so naturally that it will go virtually unnoticed. These are the natural steps of time bridging:

1. At a point when things are going well, ask her what she has planned for the week.

2. Listen and relate to her by telling her what you are doing during the week.

3. Move on to discussing other topics without inviting her or attempting to make plans.

   Braddock: *"Cool, give me your phone number."*

   Sara: *"It's....555-333-4444"*

   Braddock: *"Here, you save it, give me your phone. Save something funny with your name." [Braddock gives Sara his phone]*

   Sara: *"Haha...ok."*

At this point we switch phones. Note however, that even as we are going through the formal process of exchanging phone numbers, I keep things fun to avoid an awkward, formal pause. I don't want the temperature to change just because we are now exchanging numbers.

Braddock (as they are both typing): "If my bingo team says yes, then I'll see if I can get you a jersey and a customized ink dobber. Do you want red or blue? I'd get you a glove, but you have to be a starter to get one of those, sorry."

   Sara: *"Haha...blue! You're crazy, what did you save next to your name?"*

   Braddock: *"Hang on I'll call you."*

When I call her, "Braddock Bingo Team Captain" pops up as my name.

   Sara: *"Haha"*

Putting my phone away, I carry on the conversation just like before. Don't walk away after taking the number.

   Braddock: *"So, you guys are here for a bachelorette party, right? Which one of these girls is getting married again?"*

   Sara: *"My friend Jessica. The one over there in the green shirt..."*

[Conversation continues]

> **The Principle of Emotional Momentum**
> (excerpt from Magic Bullets)
>
> "Emotional momentum explains why most interactions need to move forward or die. You can't stay in any particular phase forever. It will bore or frustrate most women. Even within a phase, you need to be moving forward.
>
> Say you had a great three hours meeting a woman at a party and made it all the way to the Comfort phase, but the next two weeks consisted of both of you unluckily leaving messages on each other's voicemail. You will likely lose emotional momentum and your chances with her. Emotional momentum can work against you through no fault of your own.
>
> Emotional momentum can also work for you. Each phase that you can smoothly pass through builds up your momentum for the next one. When a woman talks about sleeping with you and says "it just happened", that's emotional momentum at work (and good Seduction skills). The whole process should happen quickly, not over months."

Note in the example above, the plans made were not overly serious or romantic. Most men make the mistake of making the time bridge an intense process with their body language, tone of voice, and plans that they attempt to make. This creates the impression that you want to take her on a formal, high pressure, or time consuming date.

When you talk about these plans in the conversation, don't make them a big deal or make them sound romantic, and definitely do not emphasize the 'you and me' aspect. Instead, paint a picture that the event that you are inviting her to is casual, fun, and not a big deal.

It's a good idea to invite her to something that would normally last no more than 1-2 hours so there is no undue pressure for her to spend time with you. You don't have to adhere to this once you are on the date, but when setting the time bridge, it's crucial that her mind is looking for reasons why she should go, rather than reasons why she shouldn't.

Making plans with something like, "we should go on a picnic and then go sailing next Thursday," is not ideal. This time bridge will only work if she is really into you, or sees you as a target for free stuff, as it asks for a huge time commitment on her part (not to mention that it can seem like you are trying too hard, particularly for someone she just met). It's best to save long and formal dates like this for women who you are already sleeping with.

As in the above example, after you exchange numbers, always change the subject and continue the conversation. You are not a Navy Seal team and the phone number is not a hostage that you are trying to extract. It's just a logistical tool to see her again. If you leave immediately after you exchange numbers, it cheapens the encounter and may make her feel like you had an agenda (i.e. that you only wanted her phone number as a 'trophy' and weren't really interested in her). If you were truly enjoying the encounter, then the number would just be a natural part of the process (not just an end result) and you would likely continue your conversation past the exchange of phone numbers. Also, remember that the further along that you are in the Emotional Progression Model, the more solid the phone number is going to be. If you want to see her again, it's to your advantage to stay and get as far into the model as possible.

> **TIP:** The more interest a girl gives you (i.e. the further along you are in the Emotional Progression Model) the more real and specific you can make the plans.
>
> If, on the other hand, the girl seems attracted but you are not sure that she would be willing to set specific plans, then keep the plans loose and non-specific. This alleviates any anxiety or feelings of being pressured by a guy she's not sure about yet.

Solidifying the Connection

In the above example, I solidified the connection by making the statement:

> *"You know what, I usually hate the idea of meeting someone in a bar, but you are actually cool."*

By saying this, I give her the feeling that I don't go out every night and pull a hundred numbers. It makes the meeting seem more unique and real to her.

A respected member of The Attraction Forums uses a similar technique:

Brad: *"This is weird, you make me want to break my rule."*

Girl: *"What rule?"*

Brad: *"I promised myself that I would not take phone numbers from girls I meet in bars or clubs anymore. But you're pretty cool, you're making me want to break my rule."*

It is important to note that solidifying the connection does not mean making low value comments that over compliment her, or that make you seem desperate and insincere. Telling her that you have never met a woman like her or that you never meet anyone (in general), will set off red flags in her mind. Solidifying the connection should be extremely subtle. It doesn't mean that you necessarily like her or that you expect a relationship. It simply means that she has piqued your interest because she is different and you want to get to know her.

Peer Group Approval

To a woman, her friends' approval of the men she dates is much more important than it is for us. Ideally, her friends should be excited that she met you and that you both may meet up some time in future. Having her friends pushing her to go on a date with you will greatly increase your chances of meeting up with her for a second time.

You can learn more about how to win peer group approval in Chapter 9 of Magic Bullets. Here is an excerpt:

I pro-actively find ways to bring value to her friends through such things as; making them laugh, talking about their areas of interest and expertise, or implying that I will introduce them to people they would like to meet. For example, to a single man in a group, I might talk about a female friend who might be joining me later who I'd love to introduce him to, because he seems 'cool' based on specific qualities, which I mention I've noticed about him. You can nearly always bond with men over sports, cars, or certain television shows or movies. You can bond with most women over popular culture, fashion, celebrity gossip, or by using a toned-down version of the techniques from earlier chapters of this book. Once there is mutual attraction and some comfort with a woman I'm interested in, I usually look for an opportunity to state my interest in her to her friends. I don't want to do this right in front of her, so I'll wait until she goes to the restroom or to get a drink or is otherwise removed from the conversation. I will usually say something like "So tell me about [woman's name]?" or "[Woman's name] seems pretty interesting; what's the catch?" This makes my interest in her unambiguous.

Set Frames of Expectation and Congruence

Frames are the context or underlying assumptions behind different situations. By changing the context of a situation or conversation, you change its meaning. For example, accusing a girl of hitting on you by jokingly saying, "stop trying to get into my pants", implicitly sets the frame that she is the one trying to seduce you.

You can set frames as you get her phone number so that she acts in a certain way when you next text or call her. For example, just before you finish typing the number, you can smile and say:

> *"You're not one of those girls that are really cool when you meet them, but a complete weirdo or really flaky on the phone are you?" (Source: The Attraction Forums)*

She will obviously say that she is 'not like that'. Consequently, when you do call, she will want to be congruent with the frame that you set for her. Mr. M has a similar line which often triggers a woman into wanting to engage in vibrant text message banter:

> *"I'll text you... but are you as funny over text as you are in person?"*

Asking For the Phone Number

Looking again at the conversation with Sara, you may have noticed that there wasn't a specific, special 'line' used to ask for her number.

The best way to request a number is to ask for it as though it's implied she is going to give it to you. Making a big deal out of asking for a woman's number sub-communicates that you aren't sure if you're the kind of guy that deserves it. Don't be weak, but avoid being cocky as well. Simply ask her to give you her number in the same way that you would ask someone to "pass the salt" at dinner. You'll find that by assuming she will give it to you and exerting confidence is usually enough.

Make Sure that She has Your Phone Number

You may have also noticed in the example of the conversation with Sara, I programmed my number into her phone (and vice versa). Having my name and number programmed into her phone is very important. Many women won't answer the phone if they don't know who is calling. Make sure you put your name into her phone so she knows that it's you when you call or text her.

Ideally, when you do this, you should set up more Callback Humor by saving your name as "[Name] Great Ass" or "[Name] Cute American Boy" or anything else that is playful and relevant. This way, when her phone rings or she receives a text, she laughs when she sees the name and it doesn't show up on her phone as an unknown number. (See Chapter 2 for a detailed explanation of Callback Humor).

> ### What if She is Drinking or Drunk When You Meet?
>
> If she's drinking address it. Tease her about how she won't remember anything because she's drunk or playfully pretending that you guys would have so much fun together, but she had to ruin it by being drunk and making it so it would be weird when you call.
>
> Why do you do this?
>
> The trick is to bait her into trying to convincing you that she is not really that drunk and that she really is into you and can't wait to hear from you. After she has said that, it is much harder for her to be flaky.
>
> The caveat is that you don't want to do this unless the woman actually is drunk. This strategy will simply annoy her if she has only had a drink or two.

Text Her While She's Standing In Front Of You

One of the best ways to better solidify a number is getting the text messages going while you are still in the middle of talking to the woman. Once you've taken the woman's phone number, go back to normal conversation. A minute or two later, pull your phone out and text the woman (while she's in front of you) something funny and flirtatious, waiting for her to notice her phone buzz.

Once she reads your text, she will usually laugh and text you something back. This can go on all night without either of you actually acknowledging it verbally. This builds great conspiracy, it's a great way to role play, and by the time you leave the venue you already have a 15 message text chain. This is much more powerful than waiting two days and hoping she remembers you. When you text her that next day, it's simply a continuation of the text chain that you already have going from the night before.

The more attraction and physical escalation you have at the time, the more risk you can take with these texts. The less attraction you have, the more you should focus on keeping them light and fun. Use this as an opportunity to compliment her, tease her, or both. I personally like to mismatch it with what we are actually talking about. If we are talking about something more serious, I will text her something light and teasing to give her a different emotion. If I'm teasing her fairly hard, I'll use it as an opportunity to slip in a real, yet light statement of interest. If she is allowing heavy physical escalation, I will use it as a light statement of intent.

Let's look at a few examples of how I might initiate using this technique:

(Light Flirtatious Tease)
Braddock: "This really sexy girl from Ohio won't stop flirting with me, what should I do?"

Or..

(Light Compliment/Statement of Interest)
Braddock: "You have a sexy smile... :)"

Or..

(Light Statement of Intent)
Braddock: "Kinda want to make out with you right now, Ohio... :)"

Key Points of this Chapter

- A phone number is not a date; it is merely a chance at a date.

- The most beautiful women get approached regularly and give their phone numbers out reasonably often. You have no idea what is going on in their lives, so don't be discouraged if a phone number doesn't lead anywhere.

- Have an 'abundance' mindset and view each number simply as a chance to practice.

- Having a solid interaction when you first meet her is the best way to solidify a number.

- To have a good chance of seeing her again, try to establish at least some level of comfort during the initial interaction.

- Time bridge by sequentially: (a) asking what she has planned for the week; (b) telling her what you are have planned for the week; (c) discussing other topics without attempting to make plans; and (d) later on, at a high point in the conversation, casually extending an invite to an event you mentioned earlier.

- Solidify the connection by making a subtle statement that lets her know you think she's different from other women and that you want to get to know her.

- Ask for her number as if it is implied that she is going to give it to you. Once she gives you her phone number, make sure that your phone number is in her phone, change the topic, and continue the conversation.

- Text her on the spot in the middle of conversation to get a text chain going.

CHAPTER 2 - BASIC CONCEPTS IN TEXT AND PHONE GAME

IN THIS CHAPTER:

- Mindsets and Setting Realistic Expectations

- Callback Humor
  - In Voicemail
  - In Text Messages

- Seeding Callback Humor during the Initial Interaction

- Avoid Overusing Callback Humor on the Same Topic

- Developing Your Callback Humor Muscles

- Investment Building

- Examples of High and Low Investment

THE ULTIMATE GUIDE TO TEXT AND PHONE GAME

Chapter 2 - Basic Concepts in Text and Phone Game

Mindsets and Setting Realistic Expectations

No matter how good you get at Text and Phone Game, you will never be able to convert all phone numbers into dates. Accept that you are going to experience failure and focus on increasing your overall success rather than aiming for a highly unrealistic, 100% strike rate.

> **TIP:** Remember - Text and Phone Game is just like any new skill that you are setting out to learn - practice makes perfect.

> Learn to expect and accept flakes as a part of the dating process. As you master Love Systems you will experience less and less 'flakness'. However, flakes are and will remain an unavoidable part of dating.

If you want to get good at Text and Phone Game, then adopt the mindset where calling and texting women is just a fun game that you play. Do not attach any of your identity, self esteem, or confidence to the results. Instead, be process focused and see it all as practice – the wins and the losses.

In this way, Text and Phone Game (and dating in general) can be related to cold calling in sales. Just as in cold calling, some leads will translate into sales and some will not. However, you won't make a sale if you do not follow up on your leads. Moreover, the knockbacks are part and parcel of the route to success.

Callback Humor

Callback humor is when you reference humorous parts of the interaction from your initial meeting with a woman and use it to create humor in your texts and phone calls. Callback humor is a crucial tool. It allows you to make statements instead of asking questions, show an intelligent and creative side of your personality, and bring the woman back to the emotional state that she was in when she first met you.

> Callback humor is not meant to be the backbone of a conversation. Callback humor should be seen as the spice that adds flavor to a conversation.

Using Callback Humor in Voicemail

After meeting a woman and getting her phone number, most guys would leave something similar to the following voice mail:

> "Hey Laura, this is Jason. It was great meeting you last night at X. Give me a call."

If Jason made it to comfort on the Emotional Progression Model, then this voicemail might work just fine. But if Laura only vaguely remembers meeting Jason, or did not develop a strong enough connection with him, she is likely to delete this voicemail and move on.

But let's say that when Jason and Laura met, Laura told him that she was studying to be a vet. Let's also say that Jason teased her about the fact that she didn't have a pet. With this in mind, Jason could leave a message like this:

> "Hey Laura… this is Jason. I just wanted to let you know that your ap plication for Cat Clinician was rejected because our customers would be upset if they knew that you were a vet with no pet. Haha… Hope you're having a good day, give me a call, my number is 333-333-3333."

Notice a few key things here:

- Jason did not announce where he met her (his name should already be in her phone).

- Jason was brief, confident, funny, and maintained a teasing tone.

Using Callback Humor in Text Messaging

As an example of how to use Callback Humor via text, let's say that I recently met Katie, a banker. During the initial meeting, I playfully teased Katie about being an evil corporate type. Using Callback Humor, the first text would read something like this:

> "Katie the banker! Don't stay out too late, you have to be up early to foreclose on that orphanage of blind kids, you'll need to be fresh!! Nice meeting you. :) –Braddock"

Another example would be Lacy, who was originally from Israel:

"Hey Israel... seeing as you're from the holy land, do I have to write to your parents and get your dad's permission before I txt you? It's a sin to talk to boys over there right? Let me know. :) -Braddock"

Seeding Callback Humor during the Initial Interaction

As you become more and more advanced, you can deliberately 'seed' the initial conversation with opportunities for Callback Humor. Seeding Callback Humor is essentially like fortifying the beaches and one of the most important things you can do:

- **Seeding Callback Humor helps you build more attraction.** Most men attempt to engage a woman with logic based, interview style conversation such as; "what do you do?", "where are you from?", "where did you go to school?", and other overused topics with no emotional element to them. This is boring for most women. Even if the guy does actually get her phone number, it is unlikely that she will answer or call him back. Why would she want to sit there on the

---

Callback Humor may come from:

- Topics and ideas that you talked about in the first meeting
- Social stereotypes that apply to either you or her
- Geographic stereotypes based on where she lives or used to live
- Inside jokes that were established in the first meeting (e.g. role plays etc)
- Any fact about her you can twist into a joke.

---

phone and have another boring, thirty minute interview with a guy that she has no emotional connection with?

Since most guys attempt to attract women using dull, logical conversation, forcing yourself to seed or at minimum look for Callback Humor tends to make you have more emotionally stimulating conversations. This alone helps solidify the phone number because your attraction phase becomes much stronger.

- **Seeding Callback Humor causes positive emotions to be associated with you.** Let's say that you give a woman a nickname in the initial interaction. When you call or text her and call her by that nickname, it will often cause her to return to the previous emotional state of when you met her, reminding her of being out and having fun talking to you, as opposed to whatever mundane thing she was actually doing when you called. You can change a woman's emotional state by using just a single word of Callback Humor.

- **Seeding Callback Humor distinguishes you from all of the other guys that she met that night or week.** A woman will be more inclined to remember you if you call or text her using Callback Humor from when you first met. Previously, we mentioned how often women give out their phone number. When almost all of the other guys that she meets are saying the exact same boring stuff on their first phone call or text, you can stand out by using Callback Humor.

Avoid Overusing Callback Humor on the Same Topic

Callback humor in its most basic form is simply recalling topics from earlier conversations and repackaging them in a form that makes them emotionally charged or humorous. Most guys make the mistake of being a one trick pony. They find one thing that makes a woman laugh or one thing they have in common, and they desperately cling to that joke or topic until the woman stops responding.

There are usually two main reasons why you find yourself desperately clinging to one topic or one thing to joke about:

1. You didn't run solid game when you first met her.
Let's say a guy takes a woman's phone number after a five minute conversation. Even if she was attracted and can't wait for his call, there isn't much of a chance that before they exchanged phone numbers, they shared more than base level information or a few jokes at best.
Once the guy gets a woman on the phone, he has very limited information to work with. This leaves him with only a couple of options. He can either interview her over the phone, hoping one of his questions strikes an emotional chord, or he can desperately cling to the one or two jokes they shared when they first met. If he had spent more time in the initial encounter, he would have an array of topics about her life that he could playfully spin or misinter pret into humor through text or on the phone.

2. You didn't properly seed or look for Callback Humor.
Most guys don't have a problem seeding Callback Humor. In fact, most people do it naturally. However, the major ity of guys have a serious problem recognizing the opportunities of when to use it. To achieve a high

level of success in Text and Phone Game, you have to start listening, using your creativity, making mental notes about each woman, and paying attention during the initial conversation. Most guys ask the question, "I just got a girl's num ber… what should I text her?" However, the question should instead be, "What did I talk with her about?"

For example, you may have spoken to her about the following topics:

- Where you met
- What she does for fun
- Where she is from
- What she likes and dislikes
- What you teased her about
- What she was wearing (particularly if there was something that stood out)
- What funny or sexual topics were discussed in the initial interaction

Considering these details can greatly assist you in developing and using Callback Humor. If you think about just a few of these, you should have more than enough material to develop Callback Humor for an individual woman.

Developing Your Callback Humor Muscles

The best way to use Callback Humor is to recall various topics, ideas and generalities as well as social, gender and/or geographic stereotypes relating to her or your original conversation that you can twist into a joke.

A great exercise that you can do after first meeting a woman is to write down everything that you can remember about her. Then use the tools in the table on the right to see how you can take each thing from your list and playfully twist it into a

Tools to Develop Your Callback Humor Muscles:

Misinterpretation

Over exaggeration

Forcing her into roles or stereotypes

Acting excited or disappointed because she fits one of the stereotypes 'you' forced her into based on the information she gave.

Old stereotypes about her culture or geography that no longer apply, but did at one time.

IMPORTANT: Keep these playful and make sure she knows that you are joking. The goal is not to be mean or to hurt her feelings.
If she gives a negative response, then you have probably taken things too far too early.

role play, joke, exaggeration, or misinterpretation. If you do this exercise with enough women, you will start to see patterns and learn what is effective and what is not. You might need to do this 10 or 20 times before it starts coming to you naturally.

Callback Humor Example

Let's say you met Angela in a bar. First, write out all the things that you remember about her. Here is a rough list of facts that came up in conversation when you first met:
- She played basketball in high school.
- She is a big Kansas Jayhawks basketball fan.
- She likes bars, but hates clubs.
- She likes country music.
- She hates rap and techno.
- She grew up in a small town.
- Both of your moms are teachers.
- Her family took her to church every Sunday.

Below are some examples of turning the above facts into Callback Humor:

- **FACT:** You talked about how you both played/loved basketball.

- **RELATED CALLBACK HUMOR:**
  Misinterpreted that she was actually a bench warmer. Tell her there is a big difference between playing and handing out towels.

- **FACT:** She is a big Kansas Jayhawks basketball fan.

- **RELATED CALLBACK HUMOR:**
  Tease her about how much you hate the Jayhawks. And that if she was a boy you would be obligated to break a chair over her back and after a few beers you still just might. Tell her that all of their players were on steroids and that's why they won the national title.

- **FACT:** She hates techno.

- **RELATED CALLBACK HUMOR:**
  Tell her they don't usually play country music in clubs, but that you would ask the DJ just for her. Accuse her of having a bad experience

with glow sticks and ecstasy

- **FACT:** She is from a small town.

- **RELATED CALLBACK HUMOR:**
  Make jokes about her riding a horse to school. Tell her that she needs to go home and get to bed because she has to be up at 5am to feed the chickens and churn butter.

- **FACT:** Both of your mom's are teachers.

- **RELATED CALLBACK HUMOR:**
  Ask her if her mom paddled her as a child. Tell her that your mom spanked you in the front so that Social Services couldn't see the bruises as easily.

- **FACT:** Her family took her to church every Sunday.

- **RELATED CALLBACK HUMOR:**
  Put her into the frame that she is a virgin because of her religious beliefs (whether she says she is religious or not).
  Tell her that sex is great and that she will love having it through a sheet on her wedding night.
  Tell her that she is going to hell for being at a bar and flirting with you.

Callback Humor Exercise

Ok, now it is your turn. Look at the information below and practice misinterpreting this information, while looking for playful
ways in which you can turn them into jokes.
You meet a woman at a party tonight. After half an hour of conversation you learn that:
- She is from New York City.
- She is going to NYU for undergrad.
- She eventually wants to be a fashion designer.
- She loves the New York Yankees.
- She loves to dance, but she is a horrible dancer.
- She is a great singer and loves to go to live operas.
- She's only 21.
- Her older brother is a college football player.
- She does not drink beer.

WRITE YOUR RELATED CALLBACK HUMOR FOR THE FOLLOWING:

She is from New York City:

_____

_____

She is going to NYU for undergrad:

_____

_____

She eventually wants to be a fashion designer:

_____

_____

She loves the New York Yankees:

_____

_____

She loves to dance, but she is a horrible dancer:

_____

_____

She is a great singer and loves to go to live operas:

_____

_____

She's only 21:

_____

_____

Her older brother is a college football player:

_____

_____

She does not drink beer:

_____

_____

Investment Building

One of the most important functions of text messaging is to create 'investment'. Investment is a vitally important concept in Text and Phone Game.

A woman's level of investment reflects how much she likes or dislikes you. If she likes you a lot, you'll find that she is highly compliant over the telephone and via text messages. A sign of high investment via text is when she responds quickly or with long and detailed answers. She may also hint at meeting up. Another way to determine a woman's 'investment le-

One of the most important questions that you should ask yourself before you begin texting or calling a woman is, "how invested is she in me?" In the space between taking her number and getting a woman to see you again, this question is crucial to your success or failure.

vel' is by how willing she is to say "yes" or "no" to you. Remember, it may not be all of these. It could be all, just one, or a few

For example, in the beginning, if she is not sure whether she likes you, you may have such a small level of investment from her that she barely replies to your text messages at all. However, as you build value and increase her investment into the interaction, her texts will warm up and become more frequent and thoughtful. The aim is to gradually increase her investment levels through texts to the point where she would not be resistant to answering your phone calls or meeting up. At any time during the interaction, there is going to be a limit to the amount of investment she will display. We call this the 'investment limit'. The more that you ask for action which is beyond her investment limit, the more uncomfortable you will make her. Moreover, the bigger the investment request you make that she says "no" to, the more value you lose in her eyes.

Interestingly, the more investment that you get from her, the further you extend her investment limit. This is why it's recommended that you text first before calling (this will be discussed in depth in Chapter 3) - because it requires minimal investment from her, so you are more likely to get a "yes" (i.e. her responding).

If, for example, she has a low investment limit and you call her, she may become uncomfortable and just choose not to answer. On the other hand, in the same situation, you sent her a text message to which she replies. This is the equivalent to a small "yes", which represents an increase to her investment limit. This increase allows you to ask for slightly more investment in the near future.

Ideally, you want to keep extending her investment limit until it reaches a level where you can ask to meet up without causing her discomfort.

Examples of High and Low Investment

High Investment Examples:

High investment means that the woman really likes you. Situations where a woman would likely be highly invested can include
(a) a cold approach that lasted for over an hour and progressed through to comfort in the Emotional Progression Model,
(b) a cold approach ending in sex,
(c) a cold approach where she saw you as extremely high value very quickly or
(d) a woman in your social circle that is attracted to you.

> A cold approach is approaching a woman (or a group) whom you don't know. Distinguished from warm approach, where you have some connection with the woman you approach.

An indication of high investment is the reply from the woman in the following text exchange:

Braddock: *"Nice to meet you Jane. Have a good night. –Braddock"*

Jane: *"You too, I'm so glad we met, cutie! I better see you soon! – xoxo"*

Clearly, Jane is attracted to me and has a high degree of investment.

A woman who has a high level of investment will behave in a radically different way than one who has a low level of investment. A woman who is highly invested in you will typically rationalize any anxiety that she feels around you as either
(a) nervous excitement or
(b) her fault. She will interpret this anxiety as an enjoyable and fun feeling. She is focused on the things that you do right, not the things that you do wrong. This allows room for more mistakes on your part and she may even take the initiative to move the interaction along and suggest that you meet up.

An example of a scenario leading to a high investment situation is one where you met a woman at 10pm, talked for several hours, moved venue several times, made out, and had deep comfort conversations.

Low Investment Examples:

Low investment means that you are not sure whether she likes you or not. Situations where a woman may have low investment can include:
(a) a good cold approach that had attraction but did not progress to qualification or comfort,
(b) a cold approach under 20 minutes,
(c) a cold approach where she begrudgingly gave you her number, or
(d) a woman in your socialcircle that is not attracted to you but gave you her number to avoid awkwardness.

An indication of low investment is the reply from the woman in the following interaction:

Braddock: *"Nice to meet you Lara. Have a good night. –Braddock"*

Lara: *"You too"*

Lara's response does not indicate that she is attracted to me at all. Lara is therefore likely low investment.

If a woman has low investment, she will rationalize any anxiety around you as either
(a) an uncomfortable feeling that you are creating and/or
(b) your fault.

A typical scenario leading to a low investment situation is one where you took a woman's phone number after 5 minutes of conversation in a loud club. There may have been some connection but it was limited due to the length of your interaction.

She will allow for fewer mistakes on your part and will typically focus on the mistakes. In fact, mistakes will often confirm for her that she should stop talking to you.

You will most likely need to build investment through texting, with the goal of extending her investment limit far enough that she will be comfortable talking to you on the phone. Once you have her on the phone, you may even need several phone calls before her investment limit has been extended far enough for her to comfortably say "yes" to a date.

Key Points of this Chapter

- Accept that you are going to experience failure as part of the dating process and focus on increasing your overall success.

- Callback Humor is a crucial tool for bringing a woman back to the emotional state which she was in when she first met you.

- • Deliberately seed the initial interaction with opportunities for Callback Humor.

- After first meeting a woman, write down everything that you can remember about her that you can playfully twist into a role play, joke, exaggeration or misinterpretation. This will lead to good material for Callback Humor.

- Investment is vitally important in Text and Phone Game. Use text messages to build investment. The more investment you get from her, the more likely you are to get her on a date.

- A woman who has a high level of investment in you will behave in a radically different way to a woman who has a low level of investment.

- View low investment as something to build upon. Capitalize on high investment by going for the meet up.

CHAPTER 3 – FIRST CONTACT

IN THIS CHAPTER:

- Text or Phone Call?

- Considering her Investment Levels

- The "Yes's" and "No's" Law of Investment

- Boiling a Frog

- Phone Problems

- Sending the First Text
  - When to send
  - What to say

- 3 Common Mistakes to Avoid in the First Text

- Early Text and Phone Game

- The Structure of Good Text Messaging

- Attraction/Comfort Text Example

- Baiting for Low Investment Situations

Chapter 3 – First Contact

Text or Phone Call?

Once you get a woman's phone number, the question is "should I text or call her?"

Neither text or phone is always more advantageous than the other. The key is to utilize whichever best fits the situation. That being said, extensive trial and error has shown Love Systems Instructors that in most circumstances, texting first fits far more situations than calling first does.

Texting first is preferred because:

- The first text can be used to immediately capitalize on the emotional momentum from the first meeting, by using carefully planned Callback Humor.

- Text communication requires low investment and represents a low social pressure situation through which she can communicate with you.

- By making that first text a playful statement, you come across as non-needy and allow her to relax and play along.

- You can take the time to calibrate your responses based on the level of investment and positive/negative reaction that you get from her texts.

- She can't always pickup when you call and every time she doesn't answer it costs you emotional momentum. Texts can be read and responded to at any time.

> "I've heard female friends say they hate when guys just text. Shouldn't I just call her first?"
>
> This is a misconception often perpetuated by women in relationships or women who are really into a guy. These women wish their guy would call them more, instead of sending texts messages.
>
> A woman will often rationalize that she is annoyed by this habit, but the truth is that she is usually just frustrated because

> the guy is 'playing her' with great text game. If these same women were to meet a guy through cold approach, they might still pay lip service to this fallacy, but their actions would prove contradictory (i.e. they would more likely respond to a text message than to pick up the phone).
>
> Essentially, she doesn't want 'guys' to call more. She wants this one guy to call more, after he has built up her level of investment, often through texting.

With all of this in mind, for the majority of situations, it pays to send a series of 'low investment' text messages before you make your initial phone call. This can mean the difference between success and failure with a woman you have just met.

After getting a woman to invest through a few initial text messages and slowly getting her comfortable with the idea of communicating with you, the phone call becomes a lot less of a big deal. Equally important, once value and comfort is built over text, the margin for error increases dramatically when you eventually do talk over the phone.

Considering her Investment Levels

A woman with high investment is much more likely to pick up the phone when you call or to call you back when you leave a message (Although the latter is still not guaranteed. You may have to both leave a message and call her back). In this case, calling her is optimal.

"Yes's" build investment.

"No's" kill investment.

If, on the other hand, you meet a woman through a cold approach that didn't last very long, it is likely that she has low investment. If that is the case then the chances of her answering your call is not high. In this case, sending a text message is optimal.

The "Yes's" and "No's" Law of Investment

Calling her first is like going 'all in' in poker. She may pick up the phone and you may have a great conversation with her. However, if she has low investment and she does not answer, or even if she is just busy and forgets to call you back. If this happens several times, then it can paint the underlying picture in her mind that you are chasing her in a needy way. If, on the other hand, you send her a simple text first and she does not reply, you have lost little or no value and can still text or call the number at a later date.

When a woman does not reply to your text, she has subconsciously said "no" to something small. Choosing not to answer her phone and not to call you back is subconsciously a much larger "no" than not responding to a text message. In the space between getting her number and the first date, little "no's" will happen, but you want to avoid big "no's". The bigger the "no" and more times she rationalizes saying "no", the easier it is for her to say it. This works the opposite way as well.
The bigger the "yes" and more times we can get her to say "yes", the easier it is for her to say "yes" down the road. This means that if we can get her to say "yes" and invest in responding to multiple text messages, she is much more likely to rationalize saying "yes" to answering your phone call and meeting you down the road. "Yes's" build investment. "No's" kill investment.

It does not have a big impact to your value if she does not reply to your first text. If the first text that you send is low investment, it will not even necessarily require a response from her. As an example of this, you could send a text which is a statement as opposed to a question, such as one of Savoy's favorites - "I just met your twin". This text represents such a low investment (i.e. it does not need a reply, does not ask for her to do anything and shows no signs of emotional overreaching) that if she doesn't respond it has a very limited effect on your value and does not affect your future moves. You can wait a few days and text her again and will not come across as needy or chasing her.

Boiling a Frog

An old saying goes: *"If you drop a frog into a pot of boiling water it will jump right out, but if you put him in a pot of lukewarm water and slowly turn it up, he will sit there and boil to death."*

A woman may be attracted to you, yet be wary because you are still a relative stranger to her. Making a phone call in this environment is often the equivalent of dropping a frog in boiling water – it is too hot and too fast, so it jumps out.

Calling her first will therefore usually result in one of two scenarios:
(1) The woman either will not answer her phone or
(2) she will answer, but she will act guarded and give you only a small margin for error, where just one mistake can ruin any chance at a relationship. Having a small margin for error means that if she feels any anxiety during the phone call she will rationalize that it was your fault and move on.

Texts, on the other hand, do not require much commitment or investment and do not portray neediness. You can slowly get her to invest in you by way of text messages. The least that she will do is read the text message, which gives you the opportunity to communicate and thus build value and investment. There are also other added advantages to text messages:

- You do not have to worry about her mood when you text her
- If she is not free, she will read it when she is
- It takes far less investment on her part to re turn a text message than it does to answer the phone or return a call

Paying For Other Guys' Mistakes...

Many women have awkward experiences with guys on the phone.

Her phone rings and the woman picks up. She is understandably nervous at talking to a guy that she barely knows. Her nervousness makes him nervous and the conversation becomes awkward and stifled.

He suggests that they go on a date. She gives an excuse, which may or may not be real.

He feels the girl slipping through his fingers and tries to recover by becoming accommodating and 'kiss ass' and it is at this point that the 'cute guy she met in a bar' becomes 'the nervous, awkward, weird guy.'

She then goes from feeling guarded and anxious, to bored and annoyed as she can now smell his fear and neediness. She doesn't invest in the conversation and gets off the phone at the first opportunity.

This happens repeatedly to attractive women who get hit on a lot.

After this pattern repeats hundreds of times, she is almost waiting on guys to act like this when they call. So unless you somehow have extremely high investment, when your first contact is a phone call, she will most likely have anxiety and be thinking - "Oh no, here we go again". You are essentially getting a negative response from her because of the mistakes of all the other guys before you!

An Example of How the Phone Call can be a Problem

Peter is in a bar and finds the courage to approach a beautiful woman. After 20 minutes of flirting, he asks her for her phone number and she says: "Sure".

Two days later, still riding high, he pulls out his phone and calls the number. The phone rings for a long time. He is just about to hang up when she finally answers, and the following catastrophe unfolds:

Peter: *"Hey Casey. This is Peter. We met Saturday night."*

Casey: *"Oh... Umm... Hi. Sorry, where did I meet you at?"*

Peter: *"Umm.... We met at Joe's Bar on 32nd."*

Casey: *"Oh yeah, the guy in the red blazer? Hey! How are you, I was wondering if you were going to call."*

Peter: *"Umm... no... I was wearing a black T shirt."*

Casey: *"Oh. I'm sorry... (long pause)"*

Peter: *"It's cool. I... um... well... I thought you were really cool and I was.... well... do you want to grab a drink or something this week?"*

Casey: *(Long pause) "Umm... I'm sooo busy this week, but why don't you call me next week and we'll try to meet up."*

Peter: *"Ok, cool. Well...um... uh. . . I'll call you next week I guess."*

Peter hangs up the phone feeling like a truck just ran him over. He went from cloud 9 to the basement in less than one minute. It was clear from her tone that any attraction that might have existed when he took the number was now gone. He knows that calling her 'next week' will be a complete waste of time. She only said it to avoid awkwardness and will most likely avoid his call or make up another excuse if she does accidentally answer.

If you are new to the dating game then you most likely gave a painful, sympathetic nod at the above train wreck. If you are a seasoned veteran who has been playing this game for a while, you most likely shook your head and laughed at the glaring rookie mistakes.

What does the veteran know that the rookie does not? Have you ever seen a baseball movie where the veteran pitcher shakes his head when the rookie hangs a curveball to a batter that was down 0 balls and 2 strikes? Then the next frame is the batter hitting a homerun and the rookie pitcher looking into the dugout perplexed. The veteran pitcher knows from experience that when you are way ahead there is no point in taking unnecessary risks. The smartest pitch he could have thrown in that situation was low and away. This pitch by no means guarantees success, but at minimum he'll be no worse off than the pitch before.

Just like the rookie pitcher who took an unnecessary risk by throwing the batter an easy pitch to hit, the rookie Peter made a similar mistake. By calling a woman that he had only known for 20 minutes, he placed all of his eggs in one basket for her to either accept or reject his offer in one foul swoop.

Unfortunately, women are not always helpful in the first few phone calls until they get to know you and become more invested in you. This puts the conversational burden on the shoulders of the man, which can create anxiety and nervousness. And in turn, this nervousness may lead us to make foolish mistakes and sub communicate negative things.

What if instead, Peter had chosen to send a series of low investment text messages? He could have probed for investment and quickly found out that she did not remember him, and that he had some work to do before ever making an actual phone call.

Text messaging remedies much (if not all) of this anxiety and nervousness - for both parties. It increases your chances of having a positive phone conversation in the future, because it allows you to build a nice baseline of comfort and investment leading into your first call.

Sending the First Text

When to Send the First Text?

Did you get a text chain going in person when you met, like we mentioned earlier? No? Fine. If you met the woman in a highenergy night environment such as a club, send your first text on your way home from the venue or no later than 24 hours later. If she was drunk, you probably want to text her that same night. This is so that you get her used to texting you and establish that you were not just 'a random guy I gave my number to because I was drunk'.

If you met her during the day then send your first message within 24 hours. If you met her in a social circle setting and the interaction went well, you can safely wait 48 hours as she will remember you so there is no advantage or disadvantage to texting within 24 hours.

Texting Her Quickly

There are a number of reasons why it is important to text her quickly. For starters, you need to text her while she still remembers who you are. Women meet so many men in any given week that she may forget you, even if it went well, if you don't get back in contact soon. As we have said before, beautiful women give their numbers out all the time. If a woman gives her number out 5 times per week, this means that she has 5 more guys calling her on top of each of the guys from the past. Add that up over the 52 weeks of the year! Consequently, if you wait too long and she has forgotten who you are, you have lost the emotional momentum and when you finally make first contact, you may have to explain who you are through text or over the phone, which is a sure fire recipe for disaster.

To get her phone number in the first place, you will have to have generated some good feelings inside of her. These will either
grow stronger or dissipate based on two factors:

1. More good or bad experiences she has with you.
2. The length of time between first meeting her and communicating with her again.

While time has less of an effect on emotional momentum once you have had multiple encounters or slept with a woman, it is the most hazardous obstacle along your path to the first date. This is why it is crucial that you make your first contact while obstacle along your path to the first date. This is why it is crucial that you make your first contact while you are still emotionally relevant. The longer that you wait, the more precious emotional momentum you are throwing away. This is especially important when dating younger women as they usually have a more intense social schedule and meet a lot of new people.

When sending this first text, our goal is not to sweep her off her feet in one hit. In Mr M's and Braddock's , we teach plenty of amazing openers which can cause immediate attraction. However, in most circumstances, openers should 'just open' and have no other function. In the same way, with Text and Phone Game, guys often make the mistake of trying to win the entire 'war' with their opener when they should look at the opener as nothing more than a 'small battle' (note that there are strategies where you can win the 'battle' off the opener, but they are generally less consistent). Your first text is just like an opener, it 'just opens' and initiates the conversation.

What to Say in the First Text

If you have any Callback Humor from your initial encounter, use it in your first text. As discussed in Chapter 2, Callback Humor involves recalling topics, ideas, generalities, social and/or geographic stereotypes relating to her or relating to the topics in your original conversation and slightly twisting them into a joke.

You should always attempt to use Callback Humor in your first text. Callback Humor in your first text. Callback humor has a much higher success rate than any text you can generate from scratch. Callback humor is personal to her, will make her remember you (especially if you saved your number into her phone), and will go some way towards bringing her back to the moment when she met you.

Here are some key rules regarding the first text message you send:

- Keep your first text short.
- Make it low investment on her part (i.e. do not ask for much, if anything, on the first text).
- Avoid making it full of emotion.

- Avoid asking her logical questions that take a lot of effort to answer. Remember - logic murders attraction (a theme discussed in detail in Mr M and Braddock's upcoming ebook on Attraction). The aim is simply to get her to read the text message, smile, possibly text back something short, and most importantly cement the memory of who you are in her mind.
- Avoid asking yes/no questions or anything that lends itself to a very short answer. Even a highly invested girl might appear (and then act) as if she wasn't invested if you ask – "Did you meet my friend Charlie last night?"
- Always sign your name on the first text as further defense against the "who is this?" text message response.

The following are examples of good opening text messages:

Example 1

Braddock met Laura in Vegas. The night they met, they got on the topic of relationships and what their pet peeves are. He told her that he hates baby talk, clingy girls, and that he couldn't stand the words "cuddle" and "snuggle." Laura laughed and agreed. Laura then told Braddock a story about how she stopped dating a guy who said "snuggle" a lot.

> **Braddock:** *"Nice meeting you Laura. Let's get together for a 'snuggle' session ASAP! -Braddock"*

Example 2

Braddock recently met a Guatemalan woman in Miami. The night they met, he teased her about Salsa dancing and how Latin women are bossy. He jokingly told her that she had to do what he said because he is older than she was, he was American, and he was a boy. He kept fixing her body language and teasing with her about how she was weird and always had her arms crossed.

> **Braddock:** *"Latin heat! Uncross your arms... G'night kiddo. -Ridiculously good looking American boy"*

If you cannot think of any Callback Humor, then use a variation of the texts below. Keep it short and sweet and sign your name. For example:

> "Nice to meet you Sara. Have a good night. –Braddock"

Or one that is frequently used by Mr M for a text the day after you met her:

> "Wat up [her nickname]? x cute aussie boy Mr M"

3 Common Mistakes to Avoid in the First Text

1. Trying To Make Plans

Do not try to make plans or even hint at making plans in the first text. The first text is about re-initiating contact and contextualizing your relationship as being more than a one-off encounter. You just want to get on her radar and have her reply. After communication has been established, you can go from there.

Examples of this mistake include:

> "Nice to meet you Sara. Do you have plans tomorrow?"
> "Nice to meet you Sara. Do you want to hang out Friday?"
> "Nice to meet you Sara. I'd like to get together soon, if that's cool with you?"

2. Logical Questions

A common mistake guys make, if not the most common, is that they attempt to jump into a formal conversation through text. An example of a bad interaction with logical questions is:

> **Him:** "How's it going?"
> **Her:** "Fine. Just watching TV with my friend Jenny."
> **Him:** "Cool. What are you guys watching?"
> **Her:** "Grey's Anatomy."
> **Him:** "Is that that show about doctors?"
> **Her:** "Yeah, it's our favorite show."
> **Him:** "Cool. Have you seen every episode?"
> **Her:** "Just about."
> **Him:** "I see. What other shows do you like?"

Her: "Sex and the City."
Him: "Yeah. That show is not bad. Do you like movies or TV better?"
Her: "I like going to movies."
Him: "Me too. We should go sometime."
Her: (No reply)

The example above is for illustration only. It is highly likely that if she was an attractive woman, she would have stopped answering about three questions into this.

These are the kind of text and phone interactions that every guy has with her. They are boring and sub communicate neediness, lack of social intelligence and they very rarely get a response that you can build upon, if they even get one at all. These types of texts may be ok down the road, but often prove to be a mistake early on.

In your first text, keep the questions so light and simple that if she didn't answer, you would lose little or no value.

3. Overly Emotional Texts

Avoid sending overly emotional texts about how you feel about her.

The golden rule is that you should always verbally stay one step behind whatever the woman has verbalized emotionally at any point in time. Women are emotional creatures whose mood and interests can change a complete 180 degrees multiple times in a day.

This can be confusing for guys because of the mixed signals it sends. For example, you could incorrectly assume that because a woman that you met was
(a) all over you in a bar,
(b) told you that she likes you and
(c) said "you better call me," she would be
receptive to your phone call or look forward to a first text message about how much you like her. But this may or may not be the case.

She really did mean what she said when she said it – in the moment. The problem is that her emotional state may have changed since then (it may even change a few minutes after meeting you – especially if she is meeting lots of people at a bar, party, etc) and you cannot assume anything until you hear or see the behavior again.

The way that a woman feels when she is out with her friends, has had a few drinks and has been dancing all night, is not exactly the same as the way she feels when she is at home alone in her sweat pants doing the laundry. Consequently, remember to take anything that a woman says in the first encounter with a grain of salt.

Also, you ideally want the woman to wonder if you are interested in her and how interested you are. Women love a challenge. Putting it 'out there' in your first text, or too early on in the text interaction for that matter, is generally a mistake which will murder sexual tension.

> **Overly Emotional Texts – Feedback from Women**
>
> To give you an idea of how important it is not to send overly emotional texts when you first meet a woman, when we finished an initial draft of this book, Braddock gave it to several attractive girls he's dated. Literally every girl that read the book laughed a laugh of recognition when they read this section. Every one of them said that this happened to them all the time and that they always either lost interest in the guy or found it creepy.
>
> They all said that if the guy wouldn't have sent texts like this too early and would have said something more low key, they would have probably eventually went on a date with him.
>
> Braddock explained to them that it was their fault for acting overly emotional and saying things they shouldn't and confusing the hell out of the guy. They simply laughed and agreed.

The following are examples of 'overly emotional' text messages which you should avoid sending:

> "I'm so glad we met! I've never met a girl like you."
> "I can't believe how I feel. I've never felt so strongly for a girl before."
> "I know it's too early to say this, but I really feel connected to you in a deep way."

Remember – even though you may feel strongly connected to her, verbalizing it over text message too early makes it less
likely she'll feel the same.

Early Text and Phone Game – After the Initial Reply

The early stages of Text and Phone Game are all about getting her to invest in the encounter by building compliance (i.e. achieving small "yes's" that lead to bigger "yes's" further down the road), and making her feel comfortable with you.

The Crucial Question

Before you make your next move, there is a crucial question that you need to ask yourself:

What is my goal with this specific woman?

The answer to this question is crucial for the 'when, how, and what' of your strategy for this particular woman. You should attempt to steer the interaction in the direction of what you want out of the relationship. You will push the boundaries harder, faster, and more sexual with a woman that you just want to sleep with. However, with a woman that you want to date, you will focus on hitting waypoints that build attraction and comfort and interact with her in a way that reduces the risk of failure long term.

> You should talk to a woman that you could potentially date differently to the way you'd talk to a woman that you just want to sleep with.

A Summary of the Rules for Early Text Messaging

1. Always send low investment texts early on.

A low investment text is one that does not ask for too much in return such as:

> *"What up Sarah? x cute beanie wearing all American boy"*

On the other hand, a text such as:

> *"Hi Sarah. It was so good meeting you. Are you free tonight for dinner?"*

is a high investment text, which may not be ideal as the first text that you send to a woman.

Low investment text messages have the highest probability of getting a response back. You are never guaranteed a response, but they give you the best chance of a reply. They keep you from showing your cards and giving your power away too early, and allow you to measure the level of investment that you have from her without asking her directly how she feels about you.

A woman's response to these text messages gives you a fairly accurate measure of her level of investment. Her investment is like a road map helping you strategize your next move. If she gives you a response which indicates low investment (for example, a "yes" or "no" response or a very short answer), you can interpret it as a signal for you to send more low investment messages. If, on the other hand, she takes the bait and gives you a text message which indicates a high level of investment, (such as a longer, more detailed message or one playing along with your Callback Humor) then your next text message can accelerate the meet up faster if you choose.

2. Early on, make statements instead of asking questions as much as possible.

Making statements keeps the woman from psychologically registering that she is blowing you off if she does not reply. This is because you didn't technically ask her anything. Making statements that are light and moderately funny, instead of asking questions, sub communicates many good attributes such as non neediness, humor and social intuition. Moreover, statement texts build comfort because they minimize any potential anxiety (as she is not required to respond).

Until you have a degree of investment and from her, the word "no" can have a very negative effect. Above all, do not ask her anything she can say a hard "no" to. It is very hard to recover from a firm "no" early on in an interaction. The idea behind statements is that she cannot say "no" if you do not ask.

Here is an example of an interaction that goes poorly due to the breaking of this rule:

> **Ben:** *"What up Sally?"*
> **Sally:** *"Hey, who is this?"*
> **Ben:** *"Ben, we met last night."*
> **Sally:** *"Cool."*
> **Ben:** *"Want to grab a drink Friday?"*

> **Ben:** *"Want to grab a drink Friday?"*
> **Sally:** *"I'm sorry, I already have plans."*
> **Ben:** *"That's cool, how about Saturday?"*
> **Sally:** *"I have to work. Thanks though."*

Ben is as good as done at this point. No matter what he sends next, it will be interpreted through his prior actions and will most likely look needy to Sally. Any further contact from him will also probably make her feel uncomfortable. This is all due to him asking for far too much investment from her, before he even knew if he even had any to start with.

3. When you do ask questions

Early on keep any questions so light and simple that if she didn't answer them, you would lose little or no value. This does not mean that you cannot ask her boring questions at all. The key is to be conscious of not asking too many boring "yes" or "no" questions in a row. One boring "yes" or "no" question is usually the limit suggested for the first few text exchanges.

The only questions that should be asked in the early phase are questions that are non-intrusive, yet personally relevant to her, open loops that make her think and want an answer just so she can get the open loop in her mind closed, or questions handcuffed with a statement or a joke. The more invested she is, and the more questions that she asks you, the more plain questions you can ask her without going into the 'danger zone' of going for too much rapport too early.

> An Open Loop is a conversation topic you deliberately leave unresolved to encourage her to focus on closing it.

It is important to be conscious not to attempt to build too much rapport early on in the text interaction if she only averagely invested. Not only can too much rapport kill attraction, particularly for very attractive women, but also be aware that many women will not be willing to let you get too much rapport early on. Silly questions that do not require an answer are great here.

For example:
> **Braddock:** *"Why does LA traffic suck so bad? I need a helicopter."*

> **Braddock:** *"Is it 5:00 yet!!?? I've decided that I need to just marry*

a rich girl... work is for the birds. Are you rich? :)"

Braddock: *"What up Harvard girl? Can you levitate things with your brain like Darth Vader because you are so smart? That would be sweeeeet..."*

Braddock: *"Tequilla 5....Braddock 0. I need a Tylenol the size of a hockey puck! How's your day?"*

Braddock: *"Do you have a sister? I saw a girl that looked just like you today. Braddock = said hi and then awkwardly walked off after realizing it wasn't you. Your clone = laughed and smiled."*

(To a waitress that you teased about wanting to file a complaint against)
Braddock: *"Look I'm sorry if you got fired yesterday. Your manager said he would give you a 2 weeks' severance package. You have to understand that customer sexual harassment is not a joke. We are still cool right? :)"*

Braddock: *"Hi Alana, how was your day? Do anything spectacular like save the planet, stop world hunger, cure cancer... etc? :)"*

Braddock: *"Just dominated two 60 year old men at racket ball. Braddock's self esteem = All time high. How's your day :)"*

Braddock: *"How did your project turn out? Did they give you a raise or at least an army of interns? Lol"*

Braddock: *"It turns out that I'm 21% to 23% more awesome today. :) How's your day?"*

For comparison, here is an example of a bad text that involves a question. See if you can sense the neediness and overreaching:

Mark: *"I hope your trip to Chicago was great!!! I want to hear all about it. I would love to see you when you get home. Do you have plans Friday when you get back?"*

Mark: *"Hi Sara. I hope you're having an amazing day gorgeous. How is work?"*

> **Mark:** *"Hi Jamie. Just thinking about you. Would you like to go see the new Twilight movie this week? I remember you mentioned it."*

The Structure of Good Text Messaging

The usual progression of good text messaging is:

1. Re-initiate mutual contact
2. Maintain or build attraction
3. Maintain or build comfort
4. Increase the frequency and intensity of mutual communication
5. Go for the meet up

These stages will be reviewed below:

1) Re-initiating mutual contact

1) Keep your first text short and sweet.
2) Use Callback Humor from your initial encounter.
3) Make it low investment for her.

2) Building Attraction

While how to build attraction through text will be covered in great detail in later chapters, this section will cover some of the basic essentials of attraction building through text messages.

The phone should be viewed as a mini Emotional Progression Model. This means that you need to spend time building and/ or maintaining both attraction and comfort. Comfort without attraction is a one-way ticket to the friend zone. Attraction without comfort can make meeting up with her unlikely. You need both.

Attraction can be both created and lost in an instant. This creates a precarious situation when you are trying to build attraction through a medium such as text messaging. Because you cannot read a woman's sub communications or see how she responds to your text, if you do accidentally cross an investment limit, it is far more difficult to realize and apply corrective measures in real time. In other words, you have no idea if the last text helped or hindered your situation until she responds and can do nothing about it until she does. Due to this time lag and lack of feedback, unless you are extremely calibrated or have a high level of investment from her, it is better to do most of your attraction work in person (i.e. when you first met). Consequently, at a basic level, you should be looking to simply not lose value and maintain whatever attraction you had when you first met the woman. At an intermediate level, you should be aiming to gain just enough attraction to get by, while focusing on gaining investment and comfort in order to achieve the next meet up. At an advanced level (if you are extremely calibrated and have fully internalized the principles of Text and Phone Game), it is possible for you to create huge levels of attraction over text and phone, even prior to the first meet up. How to achieve this more advanced level of attraction will be explored in later chapters.

An Example of Using Callback Humor to Build Attraction

Amy is from San Diego. When they first met, Braddock and Amy made jokes about the movie Anchorman, (which takes place in San Diego). What Braddock does here is simply text a funny line from the movie.

Braddock: "Hey did you know San Diego means, 'whale's vagina'?"

Whether or not Amy replies or not, Braddock loses no value.

If Amy does reply, then the Anchorman banter could go on for a while.

This is ideal because it works towards both comfort and attraction. It would also give Braddock great Callback Humor material for when he decides to go for the first phone call.

In actual fact, she did text back with the message below:

Amy: "Lol Did you know that Jazz Flute is for
little sissy fairy boys?"

For now, here are some of the basic rules of building attraction:

- **Use humor.** Attraction is best achieved through text messaging by using light-hearted messages that assume a level of familiarity, contain wit or humor, and are flirty without making her uncomfortable.

Examples of ways in which you can do this include, but are not limited to:

- Role plays
- Callback humor
- Random childish jokes
- Light sexual teasing or misinterpretation
- Funny or teasing pet names (e. g. 'dork', 'brat', 'punk', etc)

Note that humorous texts with a more personal touch (such as those which relate directly to her life or those using Callback Humor) are much better than generic ones.

- **Be unpredictable and challenging enough to keep her interested.** Va rying how and when you reply builds value and scarcity and makes her feel as if she has to earn you. Consequently, do not always send long replies, do not always reply quickly, and do not always be funny. Try to mix it up a bit.

- **Never try to impress her through text messages.** Trying to relate a bunch of information that you assume will make her like you will more often than not have the opposite effect. If she can sense that you are trying too hard, you will lose attraction very quickly.

- **Use the principle of 'push/pull'.** This is related to being unpredictable. Ideally, you should alternate between teasing and being warm, and between showing interest and disinterest. This will keep her off-balance, emotional and attracted. The push/pull effect over text can also be achieved by varying the length or your text messages and the time that you leave between your responses. For examples of how to use push/pull in field, see Brad dock's field reports in his Classic Writings section on THE ATTRACTION FORUMS HERE and HERE.

- **Sexual baiting and misinterpretation.** You can joke about sex or allude and tease around it in text messages. For the most part, particularly early on in the text message interaction, the sexual connotation and teasing will be very light.

Here are examples from Mr M:

> *Her:* "I'm at home, pretty sick... in bed..."
>
> *Mr M:* "Boo. Did I give you that cough? I tried to tell you no making

out but you wouldn't listen. Next time, no means no, or I call the cops."

OR

Mr M: *"How was your day binge drinker? ;)" [Callback humor]*

Her: *"No more drinking for a couple of weeks. Gotta get back to work... but last night was fun"*

Mr M: *"Must have been. You drunk texted me and tried to smooth talk me into coming out. Lucky I'm a moral rock"*

This technique of sexual baiting will be explored in greater depth in Chapter 8 on Sexualization.

3) Building Comfort

Asking yourself, "How much comfort do I think I have with her?" is a useful exercise because your answer will dictate the tone of your future text messages and whether or not you should call her. You can have all the attraction in the world, but if you have no comfort, then a meet up will be unlikely.

Comfort allows you to metaphorically 'put the hooks in' through establishing stronger levels of emotional connection. Attraction is a fleeting emotion while comfort is a more static feeling. It is key that you build attraction before heavily focusing on comfort or you will find yourself in the friend zone. However, you should be building at least low levels of comfort at the same time you are building attraction.

A common mistake that guys make is that they will have the woman sufficiently attracted, and yet continue bludgeoning the woman with nothing but attraction material, i.e. funny jokes or teases. While funny jokes and teases are helpful in building attraction and compliance, it is crucial that you start mixing in comfort building/qualifying questions and statements. Without these, she will be attracted but will often remain painfully flakey because she doesn't feel an emotional connection.

Humor – A Powerful Tool to Build Comfort

Using humor and light teasing is one of the simplest and most effective ways to buildcomfort early.

Humor and teasing can both increase attraction and build comfort. Successfully teasing a girl creates a feeling of familiarity and sub communicates non-neediness.

Women are usually only teased by people who know her well or by guys who want her but who do not need her.

Most guys are so excited to have a woman's phone number that they would never risk losing it by teasing her. Other guys over tease and end up pushing her away.

To avoid this respect her investment limit and remember to be aware of the push/pull ratio. To much pull? You are a nice guy. To much push? You are a jerk. Find the happy medium and calibrate based on the type of woman you are talking to.

Early Comfort Building Text Messages

You obviously cannot run long comfort routines or stories over text message. You also cannot text a woman a barrage of boring questions in order to search for commonalities. Consequently, while it is true that you are limited in the depth of the comfort that you can build, the goal in early text game is to simply build enough comfort to get her on the phone or on a date. Save your deep comfort building for on the phone or preferably in person.

Ways in which you can build comfort include:

- Callback and general humor
- Role plays
- Avoiding her current investment limit
- General and light rapport questions
- Kind but non emotional statements
- Encouraging statements
- Using soft pet names for her (hottie, kiddo, cutie, punk, brat, dork, etc)
- Intermittently teasing her
- Getting her to qualify herself to you by qualifying her, then lightly rewarding
- Baiting her into asking questions
- Getting her to initiate text conversations by leaving time between text message exchanges
- Not trying to make plans early on

- Taking your time to reply to her texts
- Varying the length of messages (for example not always replying with long text messages)
- Playful unrealistic future adventure projections
- Future adventure projections

Also keep in mind that early in the game, it is crucial that you show no anger, dejection, hostility, or neediness toward her. Prepare for some women to not reply, send short responses and/or put in no effort in moving things along. When you do not react to this type of behavior, you are actually building attraction, comfort and extending her investment limit.

When a woman shows low investment, most guys either
(a) get angry with her or
(b) start supplicating, apologizing for nothing and asking her what they did wrong. Avoid this at all costs.

Cycling Push/Pull: Building Comfort While Maintaining Attraction

Once she is responding well to your texts you should focus on combining attraction and building a sufficient level of comfort to get her on the phone, while sustaining enough playfulness to maintain sexual tension and attraction. This is done by cycling push/pull.

You must stop thinking of this as, "Ok, now attraction is done, let's move on to comfort." This is not how it works. Instead you want to think, "Ok, I've been cycling attraction and comfort, while focusing on attraction. *Now, I'm going to cycle attraction and comfort, while focusing on comfort."* The ratio simply changes. You can do this by mixing up the push/pull ratio.

Remember, the push is anytime you playfully tease her, exaggerate things at her expense, or steer parts of a role play at her expense, (i.e. divorcing her, taking the kids, breaking up, pretending to be mad, etc).

The pull is when you ask light rapport questions, give light compliments, making statements of emotional interest, making statements of physical interest, or steering a role play to positive outcomes, (i.e. getting married, getting back together, being madly in love, etc).

While this is a delicate balance that must be done with the right timing, you can see how adding well-timed pulls increases comfort.

Here is an examples from Braddock:

Braddock met Kellie and they instantly hit it off. Even though she was with her friends and family she hung out with him for several hours. Because he had so much attraction and made it deep into comfort, he knew he could let his guard down a little without coming across as needy. If she had been less invested, some of the things he said would have been emotionally reaching. However, because she is willing to go there, he can as well.

> **Braddock:** *"I've got this really cute Texas girl on my mind. Kinda want to flirt with her, what should I text?"*
>
> **Her:** *"Hey Oklahoma!!! Would love to see u tonight. We are making plans on what we r doing 2night so let me know what's up. Think we r doing dinner at Firefly 1st."*
>
> **Braddock:** *"Hi Texas. Just finished seminar...I think we are going to Tao...come play. :)"*
>
> **Her:** *"Cool. I have dinner with my cousins at 9pm and then who knows."*
>
> **Her:** *"What hotel are you staying at?"*
>
> **Braddock:** *"Make it happen rock star. If we don't kick it tonight...we are breaking up...I get the kids, you get the dog. We are staying at the Palms."*
>
> **Her:** *"Sounds good. Don't dump me! ;) I want too. Don't know if I can get my friends to Tao again. I will get him drunk and talk him into it. We r staying here at Venetian."*
>
> **Her:** *"I will call you after dinner."*

(She calls and we have a short conversation about how she really want to see me, but can't talk her friends into coming to Tao again. She tries to get me to meet her at her club, but I'm on bootcamp so that's not possible. She is leaving the next day and it's not likely she can get her to ditch her family and friends late night, so it will have to be long distance flirting and comfort building until I go to Texas or she comes to LA).

(Dec 7)

Her: "What are you doing LA?"

Braddock: "Just woke up. Where are you kiddo? Skip your flight and come take a nap with me. ;)"

Her: "Aww…Don't tempt me. I wish I could! I really want to stay and get to know you more."

Braddock: "I know…sucks. So weird that I actually met an awesome girl in a club. I usually hate meeting girls in clubs. Kinda have a crush on you Texas…and we are already breaking up : ("

Her: "I like you to LA… No breaking up. Come with me to Texas!"

Braddock: ":)"

(Few hours later when she is landing)

Her: (She sends me a pic of Hulk Hogan sitting on her plane) "OMG look Braddock, the Hulk is on my plane!"

Braddock: "Sweeeet! Love Hulk. Did he rip his shirt off and body slam you for taking this pic?!"

Her: "LoL…I was pretty sneaky. I'm sad..I want to see you."

Braddock: "For real…Wish I could have seen you before you left Texas. Do you have facebook?"

Her: "Yes I have facebook. My full name is "Katy XXXX. What's your last name?"

(Hours later)

Braddock: "You've been added. I'm going to bed. Good night kiddo."

Her: *"I will confirm it manana. U need to just come to Texas. Xoxo"*

(She told me she rides horses in equestrian competitions when we met. I use this as callback humor)

Braddock: *"If I come to Texas would you make me horse race you side saddle?"*

Her: *"Haha! I don't do side saddle you ass...Bring your hot LA ass down here."*

Braddock: *"I would smoke you! ;) Definitely plan on seeing you again. Night Texas."*

Her: *"Night LA. :)"*

Early Comfort Pitfalls to Avoid

Building comfort is as much about what you do, as opposed to what you do not do. As a general rule, you want to act like a positive, cool and non-threatening person in her life, while still being challenging and flirtatious.

Some of the things to avoid while trying to build comfort include:

- Trying to make plans too early. Asking her to meet up with you too early may make her feel pressured and lead to a "no". Do not push for the meet up until she is somewhat invested in you.

- Being too predictable. Consistently responding to her messages right away, writing long, detailed text messages and trying to build rapport can all cause predictability and will consequently decrease both attraction and comfort. Although this may seem counter intuitive, a woman will be more comfortable if you seem to be at least a little challenging and unavailable. The reason is that this behavior credibly signals that while you may be interested in her, you have other great things going on in your life that are of equal or higher importance to her.

- Responding negatively when she shows low commitment. Some women may be interested in you and yet not show signs of investment.

Women do not always reply to text messages and will often send short responses when they do. Becoming an gry or needy kills comfort, and most likely any further communication from her. Most women wants a man who is confident and not dependent on their approval. Always try to stay positive and unaffected, especially in the early phases of a text interacation.

As an example:

> *Mr M:* "What you up to tonight, punk? ;)"
>
> *Her:* "I'm not a punk, jerk."
>
> *Mr M:* "Lol… not a punk huh? Apologies, 'me lady'"
>
> *Her:* "Lol! Your lady…you wish!! Tonight I am going to…"[text message continues]

In the example above, Mr M could have reacted poorly to, "I'm not a punk, jerk". However, instead, he joked about it and playfully called her 'my lady'.

- **Being overly nice.** While assuming some familiarity is a good idea, avoid texts that are overly sweet or nice in the early stages of a text message interaction. Do not go looking for her appro val or affection. Stay away from text messages such as:

Guy: "how is your day going? I hope you are having a great one gorgeous!"

Girl: "Not bad. How is yours? Sorry I didn't txt back last night. I fell asleep."

Guy: "I apologize if I got you at bedtime. I just wanted to say hi and tell you I had a good time the other night."

Girl: "Me too."

Guy: "I'm really glad we met. Kinda already miss you. Hope I get to see you this week. If you're not busy."

- Early on many women would think this is creepy and that the man is trying too hard to try to find commonalities, is overly apologetic, or overly concerned with how she feels moment to moment. Even "did you get home safe?" will not help you unless it is in a context which would warrant you asking any close friend the same question. Note that the caveat to this is if a woman likes you a lot from the fiinteraction or you are dating her exclusively. In this case, she will most likely respond positively to these text messages (or indeed, to any others that you send that break the rules). Your margin for error is much higher when she really likes you. However, if she is not highly invested then texts like the one above will do more harm than good.

- **Do not force comfort.** Related to the last point, it is crucial that you build comfort in a fashion that looks and feels natural comfort texts which feel forced or disingenuous will do more damage than good. One of the worst things you can do in the early comfort phase is send texts that assume way more comfort than you have. These texts include texts that feign you being caring, sweet, nice, concerned, etc when there is actually no reason for this. Texts like this in the early phase will kill sexual tension, attraction, and suspense. Even if it is a fact that you are a really nice guy, the above behavior will not be seen as such. It will be seen as try hard and murder any attraction that she might have had for you. You can be nice, without being weak and needy. They are in fact mutually exclusive.

Remember, while your goal here is to build comfort, you must never act weak or needy. Many guys lose a woman's interest by acting overly nice too early. They think that they are building comfort by acting this way, when actually they are doing the exact opposite. This is not to say that you should brude or mean in your text messages. You should however, avoid texting a woman that you just met the same way as you would text your girlfriend of 2 years. Being nice in your texts is fine, as long as you are being nice or positive in general, and not with the hope that she will like you the more for it.

Examples of Early Comfort Texts

- Bad Example:

Let's say you met a woman through mutual friends last night and you only had a 30 minute conversation and you can tell that she is only moderately attracted. A bad idea would be to text her something like:

> "Nice meeting you last night. Wish we could've spent more time together."

This is a terrible text to send in the early phases of a relationship. You are emotionally reaching far too hard with a woman you have only known for a short period of time.

- **Good Example 1:**

Let's say you both traded funny stories about your dogs when you first met. She mentioned owning an English Bulldog. Texting something like this to get the ball rolling would be much more ideal:

> "What up dork? Just saw a guy walking an English bulldog. Wow... That poor thing was hideous! He had a face only a mother could love LoL. How's your day? -Mike"

- **Good Example 2:**

This example shows how you can include her on random stuff from your day as long as it is light and humorous:

> "The next coworker who feels it necessary to smugly inform me, (unsolicited I might add) that their 3rd grader made the honor role, is getting a body slam followed by th Peoples Elbow! ;)"

- **Good Example 3:**

This example shows the use of low investment text messages in early text messaging.

> **Braddock:** "Hey sucka! How's your day?
>
> **Jessica:** "Grrr... my boss is a jerk! He's making me stay til 7! :("
>
> **Braddock:** "Boo! That sucks. This is why you should always keep an emergency flask of vodka in your purse...Lawyers do not operate heavy equipment do they? :)"

Increase the Frequency and Intensity of Communication

The frequency and intensity of communication increases gradually from stages
1) Re-initiating mutual contact
2) Building attraction and
3) Building comfort. It reaches its peak just before you ask for the meet up. At a peak, there will be both a high frequency and intensity to your text messages. This means that you both text each other almost on a daily basis and there is not usually a significant time lapse in between each of your replies. Ideally, you should reach this stage in the text message interaction before you go for the meet up. This is because her frequent text messaging with you is an indication of
(a) a high level of investment and
(b) that she is likely to be comfortable enough to meet you.

Going for the Meet Up

With enough experience, you will begin to develop an intuitive 'feel' for when the time is right to ask her on a date. This is usually based on the tone, frequency and content of her text message responses. In general, you want to aim to ask her out when the conversation or text interaction reaches a high point and you can see that she is becoming attracted and comfortable with you.

In the meantime, you can test her investment level without too much risk by using a technique that we call 'baiting'. The 'bait' represents a non-specific or low-pressure text, which tentatively suggests the two of you meeting up. If she is interested, she will acknowledge the bait. If not, she can comfortably move on and you have not lost any ground.

Here are some examples of baiting. The '[random content]' in the examples below represent the actual body of the text. The '[random content]' is important because it stops the whole text message from being solely about the invitation while also making the bait seem more spontaneous.

It is usually the continuation of a previous conversation or some type of Callback Humor.

- "[Random content], let's get together next week…"
- "[Random content], if we don't hang out soon then I'm going to start cheating on you"
- "[Random content], tell your interns to pencil me in for next week or I'm putting 'single' back up on facebook"

If you get a positive response back from her, later that day or the next is a good time to call and set up a date. First review Chapter 9 on Meet Up Strategies for a detailed structure of going for the meet up.

Baiting for Low Investment Situations

If her investment level is low and things are not improving very quickly over text, you can bait her with lower-intensity plans. The classic line to do this is "you guys should meet us out." The key is that if she does not end up coming out to meet you, you do not really lose any ground with her as you simply invited her and her friends to something that you and your friends were doing anyway.

Importantly, try to make it so that she does not have to be alone or invest a great deal in order to make these plans happen. Remember, we are not trying to make a woman fall in love over text message and real gains happen in person. The objective is to get her out again so we have a chance to build attraction, connect with her and physically escalate.

Here are a couple of examples of baiting for low investment situations:

- ***Braddock:*** *"We are going to the park Sunday, you and your friends should stop by."*

- ***Braddock:*** *"Sara, we are going to be at X bar Friday night. Your mission, if you choose to accept it, is to show up between the hours of 11pm and 2am. This message will self destruct in 30 sec! Hope to see you there…"*

- ***Braddock:*** *"Tina! X bar Friday night! Be there or we are breaking up and I'm not taking you back this time… I'm signing the divorce papers and fighting for full custody"*

You can still use these as part of a normal text, but the above examples are fine to use on a standalone basis. Also, it is important to note that

(a) baiting should never be overly specific (i.e. avoid exact details about things like time, transport, etc) until she commits to wanting to see you again and
(b) you should never feel rejected if she does not say yes or doesn't show up.

Key Points of this Chapter

- In most situations, it is a good idea to send low investment text messages before you make the initial phone call.

- You can slowly gain investment from her through text messaging.

- It is important to text her shortly after meeting her so as not to lose emotional momentum.

- You should always try and use Callback Humor in your first text.

- Do not try and make plans in your first text unless you know that she is highly invested and interested in you. Instead, keep the text short, simple and low investment.

- Do not ask too many logical questions in your text messages.

- Avoid sending overly emotional text messages.

- Make statements instead of asking questions as often as possible.

- Try to avoid asking her anything that she can say a hard "no" to.

- The usual progression of text messaging is:
  (1) Reinitiate mutual contact
  (2) Build attraction
  (3) Build comfort
  (4) Increase frequency and intensity of communication
  (5) Go for the meet up.

CHAPTER 4 – INTRODUCTION TO DYNAMITE THEORY

IN THIS CHAPTER:

- Explaining Dynamite Theory

- Short Fuses
  - How to Recognize a Short Fuse
  - What Can Cause A Short Fuse?
  - Signs and Symptoms of a Short Fuse
  - Examples of Short Fuses

- Medium Fuses
  - How to Recognize a Medium Fuse
  - What Can Cause A Medium Fuse?
  - Signs and Symptoms of a Medium Fuse
  - Examples of Medium Fuses

- Long Fuses
  - How to Recognize a Long Fuse
  - What Can Cause a Long Fuse?
  - Signs and Symptoms of a Long Fuse
  - Examples of Long Fuses

- Phone Problems

- Sending the First Text
  - When to send
  - What to say

Introduction - Explaining Dynamite Theory

Your ability to be flexible and adapt to each specific woman and situation is what will bridge the gap between being 'good' and 'great' at Text and Phone Game, and with Love Systems in general.
Being flexible means being able to take a quick, honest analysis of where you stand in terms of attraction and comfort with a specific woman and having the ability to quickly identify the best course of action based on these variables. We call this 'Calibration'.

Braddock developed 'Dynamite Theory' to help guys understand calibration in Text and Phone Game. It is a mistake to look at Text and Phone Game as a one size fits all process. Dynamite Theory allows you to better tailor your approach to best fit each specific woman and each specific interaction. It will enable you to categorize each of your phone numbers and pick a strategy based on where each woman fits.

The basic idea behind Dynamite Theory is to imagine each woman as a stick of dynamite. How we categorize each woman is based on how long her fuse is. The shorter the fuse is, the more attraction, comfort, and investment she has for you. This means that less work on your part will be required to get her on a date. The longer the fuse, the less attraction, comfort, and investment she has for you. The longer the fuse, the more work is required to get her on a date and the fewer mistakes she will allow you to make.

The deeper that you get into the Emotional Progression Model in the initial interaction, the more likely a phone number will begin in the Short Fuse phase and the less work you will have to do through text and phone. In an ideal world we would progress deep into the Emotional Progression Model with each woman when we first meet her. However, in reality, it is not always possible to progress through each phase of the model (or to do each phase properly) in the first encounter.

Because it can sometimes initially be hard to build value with beautiful women, you might assume all beautiful women are Long Fuses. This is actually not the case. A stereotypical 10 could be a Short Fuse and a stereotypical 6 could easily be a Long Fuse. When you are trying to determine which fuse a particular woman is, realize that her fuse length is determined by how high she feels your value is relative to hers and not necessarily by her looks.

Finally, note that fuses are not static. A fuse can go from long to short or short to long in one encounter, phone call, or text exchange. It can even go back and forth multiple times.

This chapter explains dynamite theory, examines different fuses, and what defines them. The next chapter, Chapter 5, describes in depth strategies for how to handle the different fuses and situations.

Short Fuses

Short Fuses Defined

A Short Fuse occurs when you have high levels of attraction, comfort, and investment from the woman. Women in this category are highly likely to say "yes" to meeting up.

With Short Fuses, you typically have a lot of room to maneuver and a large margin for error. You can typically get her to meet for a date, push the envelope sexually and make attraction texts and calls without fear of long-term damage from any one mistake.

How to Recognize a Short Fuse

You will be able to recognize a Short Fuse based on actions that make it clear that she has high levels of investment in you and attraction for you. For example, you may be able to make overtly sexual or highly teasing remarks and her response will either be to play along or give you a warning that you are going too far. A Medium Fuse might not give you a warning at all and a Long Fuse would just end communication for good if you made such a mistake. A Short Fuse will not usually end all communication over one mistake.

If you hint at meeting up or going on a date, the Short Fuse should be enthusiastic at the opportunity or, at a minimum, does not act hesitantly about meeting up. A Short Fuse will sometimes suggest or hint at wanting to see you again or wanting to go on a date before you do. If you ever feel like the woman is pursuing you, then you are dealing with a Short Fuse.

If you text a Short Fuse, you usually get an eager text back quickly. She enjoys your jokes and plays along when you introduce a role play. If she tries to initiate teasing you and for whatever reason you do not get back to her in a timely manner, she may double text (texting you twice before you reply) to make sure you aren't mad or to let you know she was joking.

A short fuse will likely reply quickly and she will usually mirror your level of investment. For example, if you are nice and say sweet comments to her, she will usually do the same. If you were to go sexual with a short fuse, she will usually reciprocate.

What Can Cause A Short Fuse?

There are numerous reasons why a woman could be a Short Fuse. Here are a few of the most common:

- Meeting a woman through your social circle and taking her number after you knew that she already liked you.
- Having a great first encounter and moving deep into the Emotional Progression Model.
- Slowly burning a Long or Medium Fuse down to a Short Fuse over a period of time.
- Meeting a woman who sees you as 'her type' - physically, through style, or personality.
- Meeting a woman when you had extremely high situational value. For example, maybe it was your birthday or you were teaching a class.
- Having a great first date with a Medium Fuse.
- Having a great phone conversation with a Medium Fuse.

Signs and Symptoms of a Short Fuse

Below are some of the symptoms or signs of a Short Fuse. Some or all of these may be present but one alone does not always represent a Short Fuse. These are indicators rather than absolute rules:

- Texts back from her come back so fast it's like throwing a rubber ball at a brick wall.
- You have a much higher margin for error. If you make a mistake, she will laugh it off or ignore it and try to continue the conversation.
- You hint at meeting up and she jumps all over it.
- She texts you twice before you text her once.
- She really gets into role plays.

- You make sexual jokes and she agrees or plays along.
- You challenge her sexually and she one ups you.
- She hints at meeting up.
- She asks you what you are doing later.
- She qualifies herself unprompted.
- She qualifies herself when you tease her on something minor.
- You can tell that she is worried about what you think.
- She says 'lol' (laugh out loud) or 'j/k' (just kidding) a lot.
- She drunk dials you
- She uses pet names in most of her texts

Examples of Short Fuses

Example 1

When Dubbsy met Danielle she was very flirty, banter was easy, and she wasn't hesitant to any of his qualifying questions or frames that he set. They wound up alone in the corner of the bar for about an hour getting to know each other and kissing a little and scratching his back. He complimented her on her nails and her back scratching performance. He role played marrying her and divorcing her several times. They telked about meeting up to watch the 2nd season of the show Californication the following day.

Danielle: "I forget, did we end up being married or divorced? lol"

(The fact that she text him first is an indicator that she might be a short fuse)

Dubbsy: "You are so forgetful it's adorable, however because of that, we're divorced again, why are you trying to ruin my life :-P"

Danielle: "You're trying to ruin my life, Hank Moody!!"

Dubbsy: "I'm going to take that as a compliment and say thank you :)"

Danielle: "LoL! Whatever, jerk."

Dubbsy: *"Name calling now!! You obviously don't want to catch up on season 2."*

Danielle: *"LMAO!! I do too! When and where?"*

Dubbsy: *"Nah my feelings are hurt, it's like you're a different person to me now :-P"*

Danielle: *"What if I promise to scratch your back…"*

Dubbsy: *"Fine, but I'm not going to enjoy it ;) 2347 Wakefield Court, 6pm."*

Danielle: *"Okay! See you at 6pm."*

Example 2

Braddock approached Lisa while she was typing on her laptop in a coffee shop. They had both shown up at the coffe shop separately to work with the intent of staying for several hours They started talking within 20 minutes of arriving. By the end of the encounter they had moved so they could share a table. They got very little work done, ended up talking the entire time, showed each other pictures on their laptops, made plans to hang out laterthat week, and traded phone numbers. By the time they decided to leave they were lightly teasing and playfully touching one another. Braddock texted her shortly after leaving and she replied almost immediately:

Braddock: *"Even though you have a Mac and it's a hippie computer :)… I'm glad I got to know you. Have a good day. – Braddock"*

Lisa: *"Don't be jealous just because you have a dinosaur computer! I'm so glad we met cutie…I better see you soon!!! –Lisa xoxo"*

Based on the nature of how well the encounter went, combined with her response, you can easily see that this is a Short Fuse. With a short fuse it's ok to push the meet up much earlier than you would with a medium or long fuse.

(The Next Day)

Braddock: *"I met this really cute girl at a coffee shop yesterday. I kinda want to see her. Should I invite her for a drink tonight? She did have a hippy computer, so she probably only drinks sea weed tea or something like that...advice?"*

Lisa: *"haha! You sound jealous of her computer. I bet she actually likes vodka soda...(just a guess). What makes you think she would say yes???"*

Braddock: *"Well, she kept starring at my ass and asking how big my hard drive was. She's pretty forward for a hippy...
But they are all about the women's lib movement you know... :)
Think I've got a chance?"*

Lisa: *"hahaha!! O did she!?!? This girl sounds familiar. I think you've got a chance. I think you should just call her later today....I'm sure she'll say yes."*

Example 3

Braddock met Erica two weeks ago through a mutual friend Taylor. She mentioned that she had a boyfriend during the first encounter, but she made it clear that things were on the rocks and she was very flirty. When Braddock asked for her phone number after hanging out for 2 hours she grabbed his phone saved her number and called herself to make sure she had his. Because they spent over 2 hours together, getting deep into the Emotional Progression Model, Braddock had an arsenal of topics to talk about, lots of commonalities, and plenty of Callback Humor to utilize. You can tell that she is a short fuse, because he gets extremely silly and extremely sexual in this text and she plays along with almost everything, no matter how silly he gets. Another sign that he is a short fuse is that she keeps trying to logistically escalate things. She is pushing to meet up.

Braddock: *"How are things with you and the virgin? Is the sex mind blowing?"*

Erica: *"Shut up jerk, you are so mean!"*

Braddock: [Sends Erica picture of his parents new puppy]

Erica: "Do you really think that's going to make me like you more? Nice try. But he is oh so cute."

Braddock: "Cute? More than cute. He's cute as a damn button. He's a virgin like your boyfriend!!! Shall I hook you up??!?"

Erica: "Hahaha!! I dumped him you jerk! Are you going to Taylor's Bday party?"

Braddock: "Unless it's a bible study... no."

Erica: "You are so full of shit."

Braddock: "Why cause I love Jesus? You could learn a lot from him. If we don't hang out by Sunday I'm deleting your number."

Erica: "Well you never call me. I have 3 tests on Monday!"

Braddock: "Fine, then I guess I'll delete it now, but I'm going to have to get drunk to scrape that tattoo of your number and pic off my ass... damn it!"

Erica: "LOLOL you are sooo weird!! Where do you come up with that stuff?"

Braddock: "Are you being a bitch to me because I'm black? God I hate Texas girls, so closed minded."

Erica: "LoL... see! Let's hang out Sunday. Can I study at your house?"

Braddock: "Is... 'Study at your house' code for group sex? I'm gonna go with no. I have to floss my cat's teeth... or something. Sorry, Maybe another time."

Erica: "Shut up I'm coming at 7!"

Braddock: "I'm a human dynamo in bed, but I don't know if I'm good enough for you to name an exact time that you will orgasm, but we'll try. The safety word this week will be Fire Engine. Supercalafragalisticexpealaocious is just not working out for me. It's not that it's too long, it just reminds me of my ex wife.

Erica: *"LOLOL. That's not what I meant! Vicki said she wants to come too."*

Braddock: *"So many 3some jokes going through my mind, but I'm not into toilet humor. You guys have to bring cookies... And GOD HELP YOU IF THEY ARE CHOCLATE CHIP OR PEANUT BUTTER!!!"*

Braddock: *"I hate chocolate chip cookies and peanut butter cookies slightly more than terrorism... but just slightly."*

Erica: *"Haha... fine. Do you like snicker doodle?"*

Braddock: *"If snicker doodle cookies were a girl... I would call them a 6, if I was drunk. I would make out with her, but she would never meet mom."*

Erica: *"lololol... OMG!!!! Who are you? What kind do you like?"*

Braddock: *"Who am I? 2 weeks of marriage and 5 kids and you still don't know me? That's exactly why I need this break. Well that and the fact that you have crooked teeth and cankles... Oatmeal Raisin, sugar, etc..."*

Erica: *"HAHAHA!!!!! Cankles!!! I don't think sooo and you know I have perfect teeth. You told me you loved them when we met."*

Braddock: *"I was drunk and just trying to get you to bake me cookies."*

Erica: *"LOL... well I guess it worked."*

Braddock: *"Ok, my thumbs are starting to hurt, I'm getting carpel tunnel. I'd call you later, but my throat clinches up and I get all nervous on the phone with girls so I'll just hide behind my text messages until I see you Sunday. Do we actually have to hang out or can you just drop the cookies off on the porch?"*

Erica: *"HAHA... just tell them how pretty they are. Probably shouldn't mention cankles and bad teeth. Just a start. I'll put them in the mailbox... see you Sunday brat."*

Example 4 (by Big Business, Love Systems Instructor)

Big Business approached Tracy at a bar. Things escalated quickly and she might have come home with him that night, but her friend proved to be an obstacle and he put them both in a taxi and texted her the next day:

Big Business: *"I bet you forgot everything I told you last night."*

Tracy: *"Who is this? jk :) !"*

Big Business: *"Good one. Ask your friend. Unlike you, she does not have the memory of a goldfish."*

Tracy: *"I did not forget everything! I remember your necklace and crazy hair."*

Big Business: *"I've got no idea who you are talking about. I was the guy from Sudan with the cowboy hat who hated the Irish."*

Tracy: *"Oh dear. Seems I got my jews confused."*

Big Business: *"We do all look alike."*

Tracy: *"What're you doing today?"*

Big Business: *"Bombing around, with breaks for food, booze and maybe a nap (living large!)."*

Tracy: *"Hmm. Bombing around. How very... unibomber of you."*
Big Business: *"We're not unibombing. We're hitting multiple locations. We're polybombing."*

Tracy: *"Industrious and terroristic-ally inclined? And I thought your Buffy knowledge was impressive."*

Big Business: *"If you're impressed by that, I'm going to blow your mind with my 20 minute speech on clitoral stimulation."*

Tracy: *"HA! I would be more impressed by knowledge of crappy reality shows."*

Big Business: *"Is that what you're into? I'm lowering your grade to a B-."*
Tracy: *"Says the Buffyphile."*

Big Business: *"Exactly. I'm awesome."*

Tracy: *"Apparently, because my friend said I tried to sexually assault you last night."*

Big Business: *"I'm terrified that you'll try and rape me when I see you tonight. I bought some mace and a self defense pamphlet, so watch out."*

Medium Fuses

Medium Fuse Defined

The majority of phone numbers will start as a Medium Fuse. A Medium Fuse is a woman who, for whatever reason, is still unsure about how much she likes you. Depending on how you take the interaction forward, a Medium Fuse can quickly become a Short Fuse or a Long Fuse.

How to Recognize a Medium Fuse

A Medium Fuse can be recognized by the simple fact that you still have to work out where you stand with the woman. With a Short Fuse it will be very obvious that the woman is interested in you. On the other hand, with a Long Fuse it will usually be obvious that the woman has little or no interest in furthering a relationship. With a Medium Fuse you may see signs and symptoms of both Short Fuses and Long Fuses. Medium Fuses will allow a moderate margin of error on your part.

It should be noted that the majority of cold approach phone numbers will still start out as Medium Fuses even if you ran great game. This is because there will usually be a natural level of initial discomfort a woman will feel while getting to know someone new.

What Can Cause a Medium Fuse?

There are numerous reasons why a woman could be a Medium Fuse. Here are some of the most common situations in which Medium Fuses occur:

- Meeting a woman through your social circle and taking her number after only a brief interaction.
- Having a decent first encounter through a cold approach but not qualify her properly and/or building much comfort.
- She was a Short Fuse but you waited too long to text or call her, so now the emotional momentum has dissipated and she is not sure if she is still interested.
- Having a great first text or phone interaction with a Long Fuse.

Signs and Symptoms of a Medium Fuse

Below are some of the symptoms or signs of a Medium Fuse.
Some or all of these may be present but one alone does not always represent a Medium Fuse. These are indicators rather than absolute rules:

- *She may flirt with you and return your texts, but is resistant to big plans or meet ups.*
- *She may laugh at your jokes, but is not over eager to return the humor or play along with role plays.*
- *You may feel like you are making ground one minute and then the next feel like you have messed up because she just stops replying.*
- *She may return every text or answer every phone call, but she will never initiate one.*
- *She returns every text relatively quickly, but she puts very little thought or effort into her responses.*
- *She will return texts and even be playful when replying, but she will not answer her phone when you call.*
- *She is nice on the phone and somewhat playful, but you get the sense that if you stopped talking she would come up with a reason to get off the phone.*
- *You can tell that she is somewhat interested but she is a little reserved.*
- *She will initiate conversations with texts, but when you reply she takes long periods of time to reply.*
- *She will reply to any text you send and answer phone calls, but when you hint at meeting up she gives vague answers or will not commit to a solid day for a date.*
- *When you try to bait her into things sexually or tease her, she ignores it or changes the subject.*
- *You can tell that even if you pushed slightly for a date, or acted slightly sexual or overly interested, she would lose interest.*

- *Any pet name she uses for you always has more of a friend connotation than a romantic or flirtatious con
notation.*

Examples of Medium Fuses

Example 1 (by Big Business, Love Systems Instructor)

Big Business met Rachael after seeing a comedy show and invited her to join him at a friend's July 4th party a few nights later. One of the inside jokes they had was that she would constantly roll her eyes at things.

Big Business: "Let's get a few drinks in you on Friday before you start rolling your eyes again."

Rachael: "Will there be fireworks?"

Big Business: "Only if there's some sort of national holiday."

Rachael: "I guess we're in luck then."

Big Business: "Meet me in Queens for a pre-party drink around 7."

Rachael: "Queens? You've got to be kidding me."

Big Business: "You need to get into Queens. It's the hot shit."

Rachael: "Maybe I'll see you when you think you can handle a real neighborhood."

Big Business: "Good burn! I'm impressed. Did someone else write that for you?"

Big Business: "Meet me at *blank* bar in the East Village at 8:00."

Rachael: "Are you buying me food, or shall we say 8:30 so I can get a slice of pizza first?"

Subtext: Are you a loser who is going to pay for my attention?

Big Business: "8:30's fine."

Subtext: No.

Rachael: "Cheapskate."

Big Business: "I ate already."

She met Big Business at the bar and made out with him a bit at the party. Later she dragged him to one of her friends' parties where he was able to take things much further.

Example 2 (by Big Business, Love Systems Instructor)

Big Business had set up a day 2 with June after meeting her on the street and immediately going to a bar with her. There was some physical escalation, but they didn't get any further that night. She cancelled on a second meet up on account of having to suddenly move. He felt he had lost some value in her eyes and wanted to build up attraction again.

Big Business: "Hey homeless. You finish moving yet?"

June: "HA! Just at work now, then going home to organize my room."

Big Business: "I can't imagine it'll take you that long to organize the cardboard box you are now living in. Or…by 'room' do you mean 'dark alley'?"

June: "It'll be fine once I get some vapor wick candles or something. Make it smell nice."

Big Business: "I'm sure it'll be a lovely little spot to shout obscenities at pedestrians from while wearing pants made of old newspapers."

June: "What're you doing Sunday?"

Big Business: "Let's get a drink. I'd say dinner, but I don't know any soup kitchens that are open on Sunday."

Example 3

Mr. M met Kate at a night club. He achieved attraction and proceeded to physically escalate. There was at least some investment built during the interaction, but this falls into the Medium Fuse category because she was pulled away by her friends before Mr M could qualify her or run any comfort. Note that Kate is also a promoter that works for the club.

The following text messages take place over several weeks and show the value in persistence and slowly building up investment with Medium Fuses.

Mr M: "Hey Kate x Mr M"

Kate: "Hello Mr. M. Sorry I left in a rush last night :-) x"

Mr M: "Thats k Houdini. What you up to?"

There was no response to this text message until the next day.

Kate: "Mr M…how was your weekend? x"

Mr M: "Awesome. Partied with some mates from the US and bought a massive fish tank. You? Ps do you like dave matthews band?"

Kate: "Yeh daddy [this is Callback Humor – a joke based on the initial interaction], I like some of their tracks. Do you?"

Mr M: "Who's your daddy lol. I love the song crash. Just wrote a song, sounds heaps like dave matthews might record this one. Fish tank – goldfish or Siamese fighting fish?"

Kate: "Ur ma daddy…cool you'll have to let me hear it, um Siamese fighting fish."

Mr M: "Ok. I'll let you hear the song ONLY if you tell me what you really think – no BS. Daddy knows when you're lying anyway and will spank you if you do."

At this point Mr M called her and they spoke. She was polite but not overly receptive. The next day:

Mr M: "Hey girl :), good luck on your big test tonight, go get 'em and let me know how you do."

Kate: "Hi, thanks for your well wishes, it went okish :-p I'll be on the fish case tonight, ha! X"

Mr M: *"I'm sure it was awesome...I get a private performance so I can swoon/laugh/cry right lol? Talking about fish case, check out my facebook tiger."*

Kate: *"Hey hey...how u doing? Are u out tonight (that's probably a silly question!) we need to talk fish. X"*

Mr M: *"Fosho, tonight Im at cafe de paris. I'll discount my usual charge for hanging out if you give me quality fish convo lol...did you see the pics on FB?"*

Kate: *"I did indeed, looks cool found the most wkd fish website, but is based in LA! I'm going to 24 tonight 4 a friends bday,but perhaps see u at some point if ur lucky!"*

Mr M: *"Two awesome club magicians are coming w entourage tonight. Who's the lucky one again...I'm going to LA soon so what's the website fish girl lol?"*

There was no response and she did not come to Café de Paris.

Mr M: *"How was the party tiger?"*

Kate: *"Party was good thanks, are u awake still?"*

Mr M: *"Uh huh. I think I'm nocturnal. Isn't it past your bedtime."*

Kate: *"It is really, but I'm on the train. Will u entertain me on the phone plz?!"*

Kate: *"pretty please, with sugar on top...and a cherry??"*

Mr M: *"Cherry, hot chocolate and whipped cream? Ok, I'll call you in a sec if you promise to be interesting."*

Mr M: *(calls Kate and a phone conversation ensues. More comfort is being built.)*

Kate: *"I'm not your rival anymore :-)"*

Mr M: *"What happened? Did the mail bomb arrive?"*

Kate: *"No, it must have come when I was working so got one of those lil red slips thru the letter box saying I need to collect it from the depot. So I will tomoro x"*

Mr M: *"Actually the red slip was backup...it had anthrax on it. OK ms 'I only ever text cute boys at midnight', why aren't we fighting anymore."*

There was no response to this text message. A few days pass.

Mr M: *"Hey girl...what are you doin tomorrow night? X"*

Kate: *"I actually really like that name now! Lol. I have no plans, y? x"*

Mr M: *"Party animal (girl) should come down to paper and leave bookworm (friend) at home. I have a surprise for you."*

Kate: *"Oh really, sounds...creepy! I dunno, don't think many of my friends will wanna come out. But I do have a rare Saturday off work. X"*

Mr M: *"Give you a hint... Its powdery, starts with a, ends with x, and goes in an envelope to people you don't like lol. Actually it's a special paper VIP afterparty. I'm buying my fish on Sat. Need a name, suggestions?"*

Kate: *"Ah, that's not nice, you're mean! Hum, not sure about a name, would have 2 see it. But I do think u should get seahorses instead! I can't sleep :-("*

Mr M: *"At tesco and we can't decide...chicken or pepperoni pizza? I will judge you on this lol."*

Kate: *"Um chicken...no pepperoni, no chicken...ok...yeh, chicken. Let's see what kind of judgment u make on that! X"*

Mr M: *"It's a bit early for your bedtime miss...sea horses would probably attack my fighting fish. Try counting sheep...or sea horses lol."*

Kate: *"I felt a bit crap earlier so just went2bed but just lying in the dark, now, thanks 2 u, thinking about pizza! Oh and just have seahorses on their own, will be pretty! X"*

Mr M: "Ok we went with lasagna instead. We're off to cook, hope you get to sleep soon and feel better. Sweet dreams. X"

A few days pass.

Mr M: "you wanna come tonight tiger?"

Kate: "No…coz ur gonna attack me with pepper spray…and none of my friends can come to protect me :-(x"

Mr M: "Lol ok babe looks like I'm safe for tonight…Its fishes tomoz, big day so txt me if you're in central London. Have fun x"

A few days pass.

Mr M: "Hey tiger…seeing as you are no longer competition, come out and party this Friday… I'm hosting a pre
party at Paper and a night at 24. I might even leave my pepper spray at home."

No reply. A few days pass.

Mr M: "We're having a launch party at Volstead tonight… Members only club. Wanna come fish girl? X"

Kate: "I might be able to, I'm gonna be in shoreditch early on so maybe after. Sorry I didn't come yday, how was it? Hows the fish? X"

Mr M then went to Las Vegas for the . However, during this time, he kept in contact with her via Facebook. After arriving back from Vegas, Kate texted Mr M.

Kate: "Hey, how are u? Are u back from Vegas now? X"

Mr M: "Yeah, took me like 3 days to recover…Love being irresponsible but now it's just painful. Wat you been up to? X"

Kate: "Um life has been pretty stressful to say the least. Not good :-(but hey. How did everything work out with plans in the US? x [She was referring to Mr M's business which they discussed on the phone]"

Mr M: "Chicago signed. Friends moving to LA to start it there coz LA and NYC are so crucial. Why you so stressed fish girl?"

Kate: "Ah cool, I'll work 4 entourage NYC when I finish uni in may then! Lol... um just got loadsa drama happenin in uni stress! The fish still alive after trip then? x"

Mr M: "The fish were still alive but said they really missed me when I got back. If you wanna work for my co NYC you have to be cool, sexy and my fish have to like you. You've got 2 out of 3 so I'll think about it lol"

Kate: "Aw hum wat do I have2do2 get ur fish 2 like me? Get a diamond encrusted house 4 their tank, a seahorse friend or just fish-sit them when ur away living ur lavish lifestyle?!"

Mr M: "Who said my fish didn't like you? LOL"

Kate: "Haha... a quick assumption I know, but they've never met me so how cud they like/dislike me?! X"

Mr M: "I talk to them about you all the time...about what you look like...where you live...the times we've spoken... the sound of your voice...so they know who to get."

Kate: "Aside from the fact that I'm not cool, sexy or friends with the fish, would it b possible 2 add (names) to the list tonight please? Are you out tonight? x"

Mr M met her out that night and then sealed the deal.

Long Fuses

Long Fuses Defined

A Long Fuse is simply defined as a woman who puts in little or no effort into communicating with you. In other words, a Long Fuse will not help to move the conversation along. She will usually only offer up conversational dead ends and worst of all, her answers leave you in a position where no matter what you respond with, you cannot help but look low value.

When you are dealing with a Long Fuse you have to understand that in her mind, she has little or no interest in getting to know you. This means that her investment level towards you and your value to her is low and she is going to allow you only a small margin for error. Making a Long Fuse feel any discomfort or making one mistake could be enough for her to end communication completely, without explanation.

How to Recognize a Long Fuse

A Long Fuse can be recognized by the fact that texts and calls are either
(a) not responded to at all or
(b) only responded to intermittently (for example, she responds to every 2nd text or answers every 3rd phone call). When she does respond, her texts are always short, business-like answers. With a Long Fuse, any attempt to role play or get her to joke back and forth is basically ignored. If you were to stop contacting a Long Fuse she would likely never contact you again.

What Can Cause a Long Fuse?

There are an infinite number of reasons why a woman could become a Long Fuse.

A woman may be a Long Fuse from the second you take her phone number, or she may go from a Short Fuse to a Long Fuse as a result of your mistakes or other factors. You will have the ability to control some of these factors. However, regardless of your skill level, many factors will be completely outside of your control. For example, she may have met another guy, she may get sick (causing her to lose emotional momentum) or she may be having work or personal problems that have nothing to do with you. No matter how good you get at Love Systems and at Text and Phone Game, you will always have to endure the occasional Long Fuse.

If you are just starting to learn Love Systems then it is likely that many of the numbers you take will begin as Long Fuses. Another common frustration is where you accidently turn Short and Medium Fuses into Long Fuses due to mistakes you make on the through text or on the phone. Remember that as your cold approach and your SOCIAL CIRCLE MASTERY skills increase, the amount of women who start out as Short and Medium Fuses will also increase. Similarly, as your Text and Phone Game improves, you will make fewer mistakes with the Short and Medium Fuses will also increase. Similarly, as your Text and Phone Game improves, you will make fewer mistakes with the Short and Medium Fuses.

One major factor that can cause a Long Fuse is the simple act of taking a woman's phone number through cold approach. Remember that attractive women give their numbers out quite regularly. In cold approach, your value can be won or lost in a moment's notice and building comfort can take time. This is why turning cold approaches into meet ups can be challenging. Even a master of cold approaching cannot always take a woman through the entire Emotional Progression Model every time. This can lead to Long Fuses.

Meeting women through your social circle does not immunize you against encountering Long Fuses either. In a social circle, your value is locked in to some degree. It usually only ever moves slightly up or down in any given moment. If your value is extremely high within your social circle, then the number of Long Fuses will typically be few. However, if your value is low, than it is likely that almost any number you take within your social circle will be a Long Fuse. This is because women in your social circle may give you their number but this does not mean that she has any intention of actually seeing you romantically. See SOCIAL CIRCLE MASTERY if you are interested in how to change your value within your social circle.

The vast majority of Long Fuses are usually caused by factors which occur well before you take the woman's number. That is why it is important to differentiate between whether it was something that you did (or didn't do) during the initial interaction, or whether it was poor Text and Phone Game which resulted in her becoming a Long Fuse. If you are losing women because of something that you are doing when you first meet them, then make the necessary corrections at the start to avoid getting into Long Fuse situations in the future.

What Can Cause A Long Fuse?

There are numerous reasons why a woman could be a Long Fuse. Here are some common ones:

- There was a lack of attraction and/or comfort building when you first met.

- She was drunk when you met.
- You only spoke to her for a very short time before getting her number.
- You left immediately after getting her number and she felt like that was the only reason you were talking to her.
- She has a boyfriend.
- You did not demonstrate your value properly.
- She was already a Medium Fuse at best when you took her number and you waited too long to send the first text so she quickly forgot about you.
- You are asking for too much investment too quickly (i.e. you suggest hanging out on your first or second text).
- You are acting too keen to meet her for someone who knows very little about her.
- You are being too available for her. For example, you text her back within seconds of her texting you, every time.
- She does not remember much about you. You did not stand out enough during the initial interaction.
- You live too far away from each other, so she does not regard you as a serious romantic prospect.
- You emotionally overreached or tried to seek approval in your text messages.
- You tried to go sexual too soon.
- She went sexual with you and you followed, but you stayed there too long.
- She thinks some of your texts are mass texts. She feels you are saying the same things you say to her, to multiple women.
- She loses attraction because she thinks or heard you were a player. She just assumes everything you say is a line.
- She wanted you for a long time, but you didn't act. Then weeks or months later you try to booty call her or act like things are just the way they were before.
- She only gave you her number for a specific reason and not because she was interested romantically.

Signs and Symptoms of a Long Fuse

Below are some of the symptoms or signs of a Long Fuse. Some or all of these may be present but one alone does not always represent a Long Fuse. These are indicators rather than absolute rules:

- She gives very short replies to almost all of your texts.
- She gives very formal answers to humorous texts.
- She stops replying completely.
- She only replies to every 3rd text or more.
- She takes hours or days to reply every time and even then the answers are weak attempts to address the content of your text, not attempts to further the conversation.
- She disqualifies herself a lot (i.e. she gives the opposite answer of what she thinks you want to hear to your questions or jokes).
- She is rude.
- She says she has a boyfriend.
- You had an opportunity to escalate at some point in the past and now she is over it and is not interested any more.
- It just went 'ok' on a date or whenever you took her number. She is not overly convinced that it would be worth her time or effort to see you again.
- There was a time when she would reply with tons of effort or even initiate. Now she hardly replies, even to jokes.

Examples of Long Fuses

Example 1

Braddock took Jackie's number at the end of the night as she was walking out with her friends and only talked to her for about 3 minutes. He opened with an extremely direct opener and there was just enough time to build a small amount of rapport, find out she was a nurse, and tease her for being from Texas, before she had to catch up with her friends. There was no time to run qualification or comfort. Although she was attracted when he took her number, it was such a short encounter that he knew it was most likely a Long Fuse.

This is an example of how a Long Fuse will often respond if you don't develop some level of investment in the initial encounter:

> **Braddock:** "Hey Jackie it was nice meeting you, did you have fun last night. – Braddock"
>
> **Jackie:** (2hours later) "Yeah I did."

Braddock: *(The next day)* *"Hey Texas… make sure you don't wear your six shooters in public… That's not somuch legal here :)"*

Jackie: *(No reply)*

Braddock: *(2 Days later)* *"Paging nurse Jackie… Paging nurse Jackie…"*

Jackie: *(20 minutes later)* *"Lol"*

Braddock: *(30 minutes later)* *"Do you guys actually practice modern medicine in Texas or is it still Whiskey and bite a stick? :)"*

Jackie: *(1 hour later)* *"lol. something like that."*

Braddock: *(1 day later I call and leave a voicemail) She doesn't answer and doesn't call back.*

Braddock: *(3 days later)* *"Nobu = best restaurant ever… just below Taco Bell. Why would anyone choose to usechop sticks? I would starve to death if that was all we had."*

Jackie: *(4 hours later)* *"ha. Good question…I hate those things."*

Example 2

Mr M took Heather's number at a high end club in London on a Thursday night. He opened her indirectly early on in the night but the conversation went nowhere. Later on in the night, she was being hit on by a lot of guys. He waited until she was not talking to any guys and then went in with a direct statement of interest and got her number in about 1 minute. It was too loud to develop any sort of real rapport. He sent her a text message the next day.

Mr M: *(at approximately 8pm on the Friday)* *"Wat up aussie girl? X cute beanie wearing aussie boy."*

Heather: *(2 hours later)**"Not much :) I'm at molton house :) fun fun."*

Mr M: *(5 minutes later)* *"I'm at Cuckoo [a high end club in London], en route to Maddox [also a high end club in London]. My night beats up your night in a fight."*

Heather: *(20 minutes later)* "I'm going to Movida. Shut up beanie loser."

[No reply]

Heather: *(2 hours later)* "Wasted!"

[No reply from Mr M]

Mr M: *(The next day)* "How was your night binge drinker ;)"

Heather: *(45 minutes later)* "No more drinking for a couple of days… back to work. Last night was FUN."

Mr M: *(20 minutes later)* "Must have been. You drunk txt me and tried to smooth talk me into coming out. Lucky I'm a moral rock."

Heather: *(10 minutes later)* "Yeah right. Anyway I believe in no sex before marriage."

Mr M: *(5 minutes later)* "Whatever. And I dedicated my life to building orphanages for puppies that cannot bark. Don't make excuses because you're bad in bed."

Heather: *(10 minutes later)* "Well you'll never know honey."

Mr M: *(10 minutes later)* "Phew! I guess I get to stay a virgin for longer."

Heather: *(12 hours later)* "Lucky you."

[No reply]

Heather: *(2 days later)* "Talk to me :)"

Mr M: *(5 minutes later)* "For 5.95 p hour. Discount for you because you're cute. How was ur wkend?"

Heather: *(1 minute later)* "My weekend was entirely void of all excitement. Did you get pissed every day little rebel?"

Mr M: *(3 hours later)* "Went to Tramp last night and got absolutely blotto. Off to Munich on thurs. Then Boston and NY on tour. You should come… should be room in the suitcase."

Heather: *(1 day later) "Come to New York with you in your suitcase? I think... not. I'm going in March. Daddy has an apartment there you see :)"*

Mr M: *(6 hours later) "Did you know the blue whales tongue weighs more than an elephant. I heart national geographic."*

Heather: *(2 hours later) "Already knew that."*

Mr M: *(2 hours later) "Stop yelling at me."*

Heather: *(10 minutes later) "I'M NOT YELLING. :) I'm getting fat on tim tams oh yeahhhh."*

Mr M: *(2 hours later) "That's about as cool as AIDS."*

Heather: *(1 minute later) "You're about as cool as AIDS."*

Mr M: *(2 minutes later) "Wow. The jerk store called and they are all out of you."*

Heather: *(2 hours later) "Where did you get your clothes from, the toilet store?"*

[Mr M did not respond as he knew what she said was not very funny and was emotionally overreaching, which gave him the ability to control Tempo (a concept explained later on in this book).]

Heather: *(4 hours later) "Right enough of this childishness. I am DRUNK. How did this happen?"*

Mr M: *(2 days later) "They should so provide golf buggies to gates at airports. I hate all this walking."*

[No response from her]

Mr M: *(2 days later) "How's my favorite little brat doing?"*

Heather: *(2 hours later) "Piss off. I'm coughing my lungs up in bed. Hope NYC was shit :)*

113

Mr M: *(2 hours later)* "I'm in Boston goober. NYC next wk. Did I give you that cough? I tried to tell you no making out but you were drunk and forced me. Next time no means no or I'll go to the cops I swear."

Heather: *(1 day later)* "Hah you wish we made out. Clearly you can't stop thinking about it. Unlucky. How was ger man land , have some nice sausage? Ha"

[Similar to the example above, Mr M did not respond to control Tempo.]

Mr M: *(1 day later)* "I'm watching my NYC pepperoni pizza float in its own grease. Wow."

Heather: *(5 minutes later)* "And you thought to text me? I'm honored :)"

Mr M: *(2 hours later)* "Well you are Girl No. 4 on my honorable drunk dial list. I felt like I was neglecting you..."

Heather: *(1 hour later)* "Touching :)"

Heather: *(12 hours later)* "DRUNK"

Mr M: *(4 days later)* "Scoreboard: Gin&Tonic: 5 Mr M: 0"

Heather: *(1 day later)* "Going to maddox on thurs for dinner etc. Heard it's shit. Opinion?"

Mr M: *(2 hours later)* "According to Mr M's comprehensive guide to London... yes, it's shit. In NYC with serious food poisoning. Come spoon me."

Heather: *(1 hour later)* "Aw that absolutely sucks :(. Get well soon. I'm having a dance ha."

Heather: *(1 day later)* "Hey sick boy send me your real name so I can facebook you :) go on."

Mr M: *(3 hours later)* "Wow. You've got a way of asking for things nicely. [Mr M inputs his real name]. Now go do your homework on me."

Heather: *(1 day later)* "Alright mate you're lucky you got the previous sympathetic message…:). There's 2 of you on facebook is your picture of a big group of people?"

Mr M: *(8 hours later)* "It's the one with the big group of people and with "axe murderer", "serial killer" etc written under interests and hobbies."

Heather: *(15 minutes later)* "Accept me accept me accept me :) I'm [her real name] with the weird last name :). Also, how's the sickness?"

Mr M: *(9 hours later)* "Sickness defeated but will likely return w reinforcements as drinking is set to recommence in t-minus 2 hours… in Las Vegas."

Heather: *(2 days later)* "You're right maddox is overrated."

Mr M: *(2 hours later)* "For valentines, chocolate, candy & lingerie all get you brownie points."

[No response from her]

Mr M: *(10 days later)* "I'm in Miami and upon deep reflection, I've come to the conclusion that everyone pretty much sucks except me. [My name] = awesome sauce. Tell your friends."

Heather: *(1 hour later)* "Well I've come to the conclusions that you're a fool :-)"

Mr M: *(10 seconds later)* "Holla"

Heather: *(5 minutes later)* "I've had three hours sleep. Fun. I'm going to new york in less than a month. Even more fun."

Mr M: *(15 minutes later)* "Don't try to one up me."

[No response from her]

Heather: *(3 weeks later)* "Where in the world are you now, elephant boy?"

Mr M: *(1 hour later)* "Sipping pina colada in cancun mexico. Wat about u dork?"

Heather: *(1 hour later)* "Dork rhymes with new york which is where I'll be in a week."

Mr M: *(2 hours later)* "You poet you."

[No response from her]

Mr M: *(10 days later)* "I'm in the arctic circle. It's like -5000 here. Where are you at doofus."

Heather: *(1 day later)* "Im in new york eating the best steak Ive ever had and im also pissed. Why the fuck are you in the arctic?? That's crazy."

Mr M: *(10 minutes later)* "Multiple choice. I'm in the arctic circle because (a) I'm racist against polar bears (b) adventure and to see the northern lights up close (c) to find the killer penguin that kidnapped my daughter."

Heather: *(1 minute later)* "Hahaha! I'm going to say d) all of the above. But especially c)"

Mr M: *(5 minutes later)* "You're actually funny. I like that."

Heather: *(10 minutes later)* "I really am quite funny after 4 cosmopolitans. No but really. That's crazy that you're in the arctic circle. When are you coming back to London? Pls they don't have penguins in the arctic circle do they? Ha"

Mr M: *(20 minutes later)* "3 days here then back to London for a while. Its cold. Come spoon me."

Heather: *(2 hours later)* "Erm no! You're too nasty to me for spooning ;) PS I am fucked! Who said you had to be 21 in the states to drink? HA"

Mr M: *(1 week later)* "You back from the big apple? Did me proud w the drunk dial txting… the wasted alter ego is bloody hilarious."

Heather: *(3 hours later)* "Yeah I'm back. Mate London is such a let down after New York. How were my texts any different from usual? Ha. Are your jetting off anywhere fun soon?"

Mr M: *(10 hours later) "Wat up punk... I'm almost recovered from the Mexican bird flu. GI [my name] should make his comeback this sat at movida."*

[No response]

Mr M: *(2 days later) "April 11, party at Movida. Kssshht, I repeat, the crips are raiding the liquor store. Mother goose, over ... ;)"*

Heather: *(1 day later) "What's in it for me?"*

Mr M: *(1 hour later) "I'll throw in a midget if you can out drink me."*

Heather: *(1 hour later) "Score. I accept your challenge."*

Mr M: *(1 day later) "What's in it for me?"*

Heather: *(4 hours later) "What's in it for you? Surely my presence is enough?"*

Mr M: *(2 hours later) "In what world is me getting your presence and your getting a midget a fair deal lol? All bets are off... I'm keeping the midget and you can have some champagne from my table MAYBE."*

Heather: *(10 min later) "haha...Fine. I'm in. What time?"*

You can clearly see how comfort and attraction has been built over text message in this exchange. Mr M probably would have pushed for the meet up sooner in this interaction, however, he was out of London for 2 months on a BOOTCAMP tour which is why he had to burn down the Long Fuse by building up comfort (mostly through familiarity) before going for the meet up.

Example 3 (by Big Business):

Here is an example of a Medium to Long Fuse which shows the power of getting a woman out and doing your work in person, as opposed to over the phone:

Big Business picked up Leah on the street while flyering for a free movie screening. He made plans with her in person, but wanted to continue building attraction via text, so he tried instigating some back and forth texts, but she wasn't having it.

Big Business: *"At work. Bored. Text me something interesting."*

[No reply]

The next day...

Big Business: *"Have you ever been to the [name of bar] bar?"*

Leah: *"Nope."*

Big Business: *"I now know what we're doing tomorrow. How psyched are you?"*

[No reply.]

The day of the date...

Big Business: *"Here's the adrs of the joint. Let's meet there at 9 pm."*

Leah: *"Sounds good."*

She was sending short little responses when necessary. It was very formal and there was no feeling of fun. He was half expecting her to never show up. However, to his surprise, she did show up and the date went beautifully. He managed to run the full Emotional Progression Model on her (which shows you the advantage that you have when you can escalate in person as opposed to over the phone).

They had this conversation in her bed:

Big Business: *"You have the least clever texts of anyone I know. It's like you put no thought into them whatsoever."*

Leah: *"I was playing hard to get."*

Big Business: *"Well...stop it!"*

Note that this could also be the result of backwards rationalization. She may rationalize now that she was 'playing hard to get', but the reality could have been that she was not very interested in the beginning. Because he was able to sleep with her on the date, she became highly invested in him and may have rationalized that all she was doing by being difficult over text was playing hard to get. and may have rationalized that all she was doing by being difficult over text was playing hard to get.

The following texts were then exchanged whilst he drove home:

Big Business: *"You forgot to show me your etchings. Why the hell did I even come over there?"*

Leah: *"Hold on. Putting some thought into my text..."*

Big Business: *"There we go! I'm raising your grade to a B-."*

Leah: *"B-?! What was I at before?"*

Big Business: *"You don't want to know. You lost major points when you tried to make me go all the way."*

Leah: *"Yeah. You really put up a fight."*

Big Business: *"Good luck getting in my pants now. I'm holding out till the 4th date."*

Leah: *"Or until I wear some cool underwear."*

Big Business: *"Or none..."*

Key Points of this Chapter

- Dynamite Theory states that you should calibrate your actions to different situations. The basic idea behind Dynamite Theory that each woman has a different fuse length:

- A Short Fuse is a woman who has a high level of attraction, comfort and investment with you.

- A Medium Fuse is a woman who is still unsure about how much she likes you. Depending on how you take the interaction forward, a Medium Fuse can quickly become a Short Fuse or a Long Fuse.

- A Long Fuse is a woman who has a low level of attraction, comfort and investment with you and puts little or no effort into communicating with you.

- The shorter the fuse, the less work will be required to get her on a date. The longer the fuse is, the more work will be required to get her on a date.

- The deeper that you get into the Emotional Progression Model in the initial interaction, the more likely a phone number will begin as a Short Fuse.

- A fuse can go from long to short or short to long in one encounter, phone call, or text exchange. It can even go back and forth multiple times.

CHAPTER 5 - STRATEGIES FOR EACH FUSE

IN THIS CHAPTER:

- Short Fuse Strategies
  - Go for the Date
  - There is No Need to Spend Too Much Time on the Phone With a Short Fuse
  - Do Not Over Text
  - Examples of Short Fuses

- Medium Fuse Strategies
  - Extending a "You Guys Should Meet Us Out" Invite
  - Burn Her Down to a Short Fuse

- Long Fuse Strategies
  - Pinging and Keeping on Her Radar
  - A Covert Tactic - the Mass Text
  - Do Not Seem Too Excited
  - Do Not Get Emotional
  - Be Patiently Persistent

Chapter 5 -Strategies for Each Fuse
Short Fuse Strategies

Because Short Fuses have high levels of investment, it is typically not difficult to turn a Short Fuse into a meet up or date. The key strategy for a Short Fuse is simply, 'do not mess it up'. With this in mind, below are the strategies for Short Fuses.

Go for the Date

If a woman is a Short Fuse you can usually ask for the meeting or date through text or phone call relatively early on in the interaction. This is typically a good strategy because not acting on a Short Fuse can lead to the Short Fuse turning into a Medium or Long Fuse.

An Advanced Short Fuse Strategy – Hard Disqualifying

A more advanced Short Fuse strategy is to playfully disqualify hard. This causes a lot of attraction because it sets the tone that she is chasing you.

For example, Braddock was texting Jamie when she was a Medium Fuse. This is the typical response that he received:

Braddock: What's up Jamie? We are going to X, you guys should come.

Jamie: I'll talk to my friends and see what we're doing.

However, when Jamie became a Short Fuse, notice the role reversal and the brevity of Braddock's response:

Jamie: "Hey Braddock what are you and the boys doing tonight?

Braddock: "X Bar. Come play."

This will often increase attraction as she is now forced to chase him.

Because it is a short fuse, there is no need to overcomplicate things. You can send a text such as:

Braddock: *"What are you doing ex wife (or appropriate Callback*

Humor)? I wanna see you soon. Grab a drink tomorrow?"

Notice there is nothing fancy about the above invitation to meet up via text message. Because it is a short fuse you can skip steps and be straight to the point. Notice how:

- Firstly, notice how the message conveys interest by stating that you want to see her, but it avoids being needy by being sweet, yet somewhat business like.
- Secondly, notice how the message is short and sweet. You want to avoid writing overly long drawn out invites. It shows that you are not taken this to seriously and that you did not spend 30 minutes crafting the perfect text message because you are nervous.
- Lastly, using a pet name or Callback Humor early in the sentence softens the formal invite and makes it more relaxed.
- Often times they will say something like, "I can't tomorrow, but what are you doing Wednesday?" This is fine. If she is trying to help find a date that is logistically feasible for her, then go with it if it fits your schedule as well. Do not get over excited and do not over plan. Say something short and sweet like, "Wed is cool. How about 7?"

No Need to Spend Too Much Time on the Phone With a Short Fuse

When you are dealing with a Short Fuse on the phone, you do not have to spend too much time in conversation. An interaction would ideally consist of making her laugh a few times, setting up a meeting and getting off the phone at a high point so that you leave her wanting more.

This should take no longer than 10 minutes and often times less than 5. The reason for this is that if she is a Short Fuse, she already likes you. The longer that you spend talking to her on the phone, the more likely it is that you lose her through misinterpretation, jokes that do not hit, awkward silences, etc. Spending less time on the phone minimizes the chance of this.

If you are not sure if she is short or medium you can always call her to get a better feel. In such a case, you may not want to be as transparent as above. To facilitate this you may want to give the impression that you are busy on certain days and free on certain days. When you are on the phone with her you can tell her that you think that you are busy on certain days before telling her when you are free. If she is not free on that day, you can change your availability once, but avoid appearing to be too accommodating. So, for example:

[After random interesting conversation]

You: *"Cool. You know, I should really go. We could talk forever at this rate but I have to run. I don't have my schedule on me but I'm pretty sure I'm busy Monday and Wednesday, but I think I'm free on Tuesday. You want to catch up then?"*

Her: *"I would love to but I can't on Tuesday – it's my Mom's birthday."*

You: *"OK, hang on, let me see what my schedule says [pretending that you are checking your schedule]. Oh, I'm actually free Wednesday after 7pm. You wanna grab a quick drink then?"*

Her: *"Sure, that sounds great! Where?"*

Observe how you made yourself unavailable on certain days, but modified this by 'checking your schedule'. If, after modifying once, she is still not available, do not try for the meet up again and do not make a big deal out of not being able to meet up. So for example:

You: *"OK, hang on, let me see what my schedule says [pretending that you are checking your schedule]. Oh, I'm actually free Wednesday after 7pm. You wanna grab a quick drink then?"*

Her: *"Um, I'm busy then too."*

You: *"No worries. We'll grab one next week."*

Her: *"OK"*

In this case (particularly if she does not suggest another meet up) the likelihood is that she was a Medium or Long Fuse. You should build value over text and phone and then try to set the meeting up again after a few days or maybe even a week.

Do Not Over Text: Avoid Making a Short Fuse Long

The fastest way to make a Short Fuse become a Medium Fuse or Long Fuse is by over texting. When you over text you often times end up appearing needy or desperate. The old saying "less is more" is very true in regards to text and phone game. This topic is covered in depth in the 'Tempo' section of the Chapter 7 on Value. However, in summary:

- Avoid 'double texting' or following up a weak text with an apology or clarification unless absolutely necessary. If you send a tease or a joke and she does not reply right away, do not apologize or ask her if you did something wrong. Simply wait a few hours for her to reply. If she does not reply then, simply send her a new text message changing the subject.
- Try to end most of the conversations first on high notes.
- Do not always send long replies. Instead, mix them up so that some are short and some are long.
- Make some of your replies delayed to keep her guessing. It is perfectly fine to reply right away sometimes. You just do not want to make it a habit of replying right away every time. Wait 20 minutes or an hour before replying every once in a while to make her wonder.
- Do not always be funny.
- Do not always push for a meet up. Every text message should not be an attempt to set up a date. Only invite her out once or twice a week. Seeing what she is doing that day is fine, but trying to nail her down for one on one time every day will turn her into a Medium Fuse or Long Fuse quickly.

Let's look at a Short Fuse example:

Braddock met Nikki a few days ago. She works at a tanning salon. He has been in there several times and they always flirt a lot. The last time he was in there he finally got her number. He always teases her for being a pushy salesman who is always looking to up sell. Based on the fact that she is always touchy feely in the store, talks to him for at least 20 minutes each time he comes in, and she started hinting at wanting to hang out you can assume she is a short fuse.

Example 1 (by Braddock)

> **Braddock:** *"if I text you just to say hi….are you still going to try to up sale me to a triple bronzer? –Braddock."*

Nikki: *"lolol…You smart ass! I don't do that. What are you doing?"*

Braddock: *"I'm at the DMV. I feel like I'm at a live taping of the Jerry Springer show."*

Nikki: *"haha..yeah those places are sketchy. I'm so bored at work. Come see me."*

Braddock: *"Already up sold everyone in there huh? Sooo pushy. You could sale ice to an Eskimo…and by 'sale' I mean make him buy."*

Nikki: *"lolol…I'm not like that!!!"*

Braddock: *"Sure…sure.…drink tonight after work or we are breaking up for good salon girlfriend."*

Nikki: *"haha…fine, don't dump me! I get off at 7. I'll call you then."*

Example 2 (by Braddock)

Braddock met Jenna last night at a club in Vegas. She was there for a pharmacy convention. Braddock used this in his callback humor. She is a short fuse because they hung out all night long. They were texting each other in the club when they would get separated and texting after they left that night. Because she is a short fuse, instead of wasting time with a ton of text messages, he simply flirts a little bit and pushes for the meet up.

(Starting from the texts in the club)

Braddock: *"This really cute pharmacist from DC won't leave me alone…thinking about making out with her."*

Jenna: *"Come back to our table and hang out with me and my friends."*

Braddock: *"I'm at the back bar.…come here."*

Jenna: *"No come here!! I'm stuck by myself cause my friend is talking to your friend. Pleeeease!"*

Braddock: *"Alright…coming your way."*

(Later that night after the club. I couldn't get her to come back to my hotel.)

Jenna: "Back in my room…bored. Should have come over…"

Braddock: "Steal a key and come see me.. ;)"

Jenna: "It's late…about to pass out. I'm all yours tomorrow…."

(Next Day)

Braddock: "I met this really cute girl form DC last night. I want to flirt with her, what should I say?"

Jenna: "hahaha….hey!!! Whatcha doin?"

Braddock: "Teaching seminar. Did you know that I'm 12% more awesome today?"

Jenna: "lol…naturally."

Braddock: "Friends are going to Lavo tonight. You guys come with us."

Jenna: "cool. We are in."

(Few Hours Later)

Braddock: "What are you and your fellow drug dealers doing?"

Jenna: "lolol….shopping all day. Getting food now. Palazzo around 9?"

Braddock: "We'll be there closer to 11. Text you when we are there."

(Few Hours Later)

Braddock: "We are heading that way….How is it? Be there in like 15min."

Jenna: "Yay!!! Paaaaacked! But good. Text me when you get inside."

Example 3 (by Daxx, Love Systems Instructor)

Daxx met Julie Thursday at a club. She was one of the hostesses of the club. She was very flirty and kept finding Daxx even though she was supposed to be working. They talked off and on all night. The next day he told her about how he was heading to Las Vegas for a night. He texted her when he got back.

Daxx: *"What up punk! You can tell everyone its safe to come out of their homes again because we're back in LA. When we gonna kick it like karate. Kev (London)."*

Julie: *"Hahaha well im at wrk soo u should stop by."*

Daxx: *"A) Don't tell me what to do just cos you're hot. B) We better hang out by next week or we're breaking up. C) I'm awesome."*

Julie: *"Hahahahaha omg ur a dork!"*

(Next Day)

Julie: *"Ummmmmm.....helllloooooo! Hahaha"*

Daxx: *"Who's this?"*

Julie: *"J from (club)."*

Daxx: *"Yeh I know….just messing with you retard :)"*

Julie: *"LoL….Oh well thanx…."*

Daxx: *"We might be coming (club). If we do you better flirt with me or we're breaking up, I'm taking the kids & the dog."*

Julie: *"Hahaha well im off already…im at (other club)."*

Daxx: *"Well we are definitely breaking up now sexy."*

Julie: *"Lol oh hush! I do want to see you soon."*

(Next Day)

Daxx: "Newsflash: I'm the best....possibly ever. What you up to trouble?"

Julie: "Im glad u think u are the best ever congratulations to u! Hahhaa..im chill at home...super tired thinking about taking a nap then going to (club) later tonight. U?"

Daxx: "I started getting some work done then realised lazing around in the comfiest bed in the world was a better option for a sunday. Me & Braddock are gonna go see 2012 bit later. That is of course after a power nap of a champion."

Julie: "Hahaha niiiice well i hope u two have fun..we need to get2gether soon!"

(A Few Days Later)

Daxx: "You never write, you never call. The kids wanna know when mum's coming home, what am I meant to tell them?"

Julie: "Hahahahahahahahahahahahaaahaha omg! U freakin crack me up!"

Daxx: "Lol. What's new punk?"

Julie: "Not to much..just wrking both jobs tonight. I went to vegas last night w/my roomie. just for the hell of it and pulled an all nighter and now im at wrk and have to go straight to my night job after..im beat!"

Daxx: "Rule #76: No excuses, play like a champion. That is pretty hardcore, there was me thinking you were a good girl J. Let's kick it this w.e when you're done catchin up from vegas sexy."

Julie: "Haha..well what are u doing tomorrow during the day? I have the day off soo when i wake up im down to get something to eat or do whatever."

Daxx: "Sounds good. Just gonna be workin/saving the world tomorrow. Come by the house when you're up & we'll go get sumin to eat - (sent my address). But after a vegas all nighter I'll put money on you not being in action til atleast 1pm."

Julie: "Hahah u are very right!! I deff. Wont be up any earlier then that. Ok i will call u when i wake up!"

(Next Day)

Julie: "Omg i just woke up! And im still tired haha! Wow! Well im trying to get myself out of my bed. Are u on a time limit today?"

Daxx: "Haha that's what happens when you go the full 12 rounds with Vegas. Just getting work done shawty. I've got to be back by 7pm otherwise I'll get grounded but other than that I'm good."

Julie: "Haha..ur too funny! Ok well that wrks out perfect b/c i have wrk at 8. Soo let me get my lazy ass up i have to take a shower..i will hurry and then come get u..is that cool? I will text u when im on my way."

Daxx: "Sounds good hottie"

(Few Hours Later)

Julie: "Ok soo i know im taking forever im moving a little retardedly slow haha but im almost ready."

Daxx: "Well even tho you're the 2nd slowest person in the world behind a legless tortoise, good timing cos I just finished what I had to do. See ya in a bit."

Julie: "Hahahah wow thanx!"

Julie: "I'm outside."

Medium Fuse Strategies

One of the most important questions to ask yourself when you get a Medium Fuse is "what do I want from this woman and how much do I like her?" If the answer is that you would just like to sleep with her and don't see great potential for a relationship, then you can simply adopt a high risk/high reward strategy and treat the Medium Fuse as you would a Short Fuse. Short Fuse strategies can work on a Medium Fuse (or, on rare occasions, on a Long Fuse) but there is a high risk that they will not work.

Although you have a greater chance of sleeping with her sooner, you also have a corresponding greater chance of turning her to a Long Fuse or suddenly losing her.

On the other hand, if you actually want to convert the Medium Fuse, there are two predominant strategies that you should use:

1. Spend some time on the phone qualifying her and building comfort. You can build comfort on the phone much easier and much faster than you can through text. With some medium fuses, you will need to call them. There is no way around it.
2. Burn her down to a Short Fuse by continuing to text her and build attraction over time by displaying humor, value and non neediness by pinging until she becomes a Short Fuse.
3. Extend a "you guys should meet us out" invite.

You can also use the three strategies in tandem.

Extending a "You Guys Should Meet Us Out" Invite

Building attraction and escalating is best done in person. If the woman is a Medium or Long Fuse, your best option may be meeting her out and continue moving through the Emotional Progression Model. She may not be comfortable enough to show up for a one on one date yet, but she might be fine with the idea of meeting in a relaxed public setting. By inviting her friends out with her, you make it far more likely that she will be comfortable enough to come because she can always talk to her friends in moments of social awkwardness and not have that trapped feeling you can get on a date. Avoiding social awkwardness is very important to women. Once you meet her out in person (whether or not her friends are there) you then have the opportunity to build attraction again and burn her down to a more manageable fuse length.

A great way to get her out is through a very casual invite. The magic words for this type of invite are:

"You guys should meet us at X"

The key is that even though you extended an invitation, it was so casual that you have not lost value if her and her friends do not come. If she does come, then you should follow the Emotional Progression Model or if she is in your social circle, the principles taught in SOCIAL CIRCLE MSTERY. Other variations to the invite are:

> *"We are having a party next Saturday, you and your friends should come."*
> *"A group of us are going to the park Sunday, you and your friends should come."*
> *"We are getting bottle service at X tonight, you and your friends should come."*
> *"What are you guys up to tonight brat? We might be going to X, you guys should meet us."*
> *"Your mission if you and your friends choose to accept it is to go to X around 11ish. This message will self destruct in 15 seconds. ;)"*

If she agrees to come, then ideally call her to give her the information. Be short, funny, playful (but not overly flirty), and try to be the one to end the conversation first. If she does not pick up, then leave a funny voice mail (leaving voice mails is covered in detail in Chapter 6) but do not leave the details on the voice mail. You should expect her to call you back.

If she says she is coming but subsequently flakes, do not get upset. Accept that flakiness is a part of the dating game and do not rely on one Medium Fuse woman to make your entire night. Instead, have a number of different women that you invited to the same event, in which case, one is bound to show up.

Burn Her Down to a Short Fuse

To turn a Medium Fuse into a Short Fuse:

- Use humor and Callback Humor. If she is a Medium Fuse, you need to keep building momentum. You are essentially trying to slowly pique her interest enough to get her on the phone or set up a meeting. A good way to do this is to increase her attraction to you by utilizing Callback Humor.

- Follow the rules outlined in the chapter on First Contact. In summary, these are:

  - Always send low investment texts early on.
  - Make statements instead of asking questions.

- Keep any questions light and simple and avoid too many rapport seeking questions.
- Do not ask her anything that she can say a hard "no" to.
Call a few times per week just to chat. Build comfort and flirt on several calls before trying to make plans.

Once she exhibits the signs of a Short Fuse, it is important that you act on it and invite her out. A Medium or Long Fuse that is converted into a Short Fuse is often only a Short Fuse for a limited amount of time. You should thus 'strike while the iron is hot' and invite her out to meet you where you can escalate further in person. This does not mean you start acting needy or pushy. It simply means the window has opened and it is now time to start pushing for the meet up with more regularity.

<u>Medium Fuse Example (by Dubbsy, Love Systems Instructor)</u>

I met Nikki once in a bar in my hometown, I had asked her to take a picture of my group of friends and we made some poses, she took a couple different pics and then turned back to her friends. That was the end of that interaction. About a month later I saw her in a bar where I went to school (different state), and went up to her and asked if she was stalking me. Took her a second to remember me, but then we had a couple lines back and forth, and said we'd hang out back in NY, exchanged numbers and left the bar. Because of this I assumed a Medium Fuse or a Long Fuse because I didn't get enough time really to solidify the number. However, based on her responses I would consider her a Medium Fuse.

What we spoke about was mainly where she was from in NY and I made fun of her for it being "upstate" even though it was only one city above my own, and different places to go out in the city I'm from.

(The next day)

Dubbsy: *"I've never met a person from upstate, kinda relieved to see you're just like normal people."*

Nikki: *"Lol, only one difference, we put our pants on two legs at a time."*

Dubbsy: *"Please I've been doin that since 86', step your game up! :P"*

Nikki: *"Lol"*

Dubbsy: *"You coming out to XX bar this weekend, they finally put the tent up "*

Nikki: *"Yeah I think we'll be down there one of these nights, you?"*

Dubbsy: *"Exploring your photography skills huh, you can follow me around and take pictures of me all night, combine your passion of taking pictures and stalking me :-P"*

Nikki: *"OMG you stalked me!"*

Dubbsy: *"Nah Nikki Mouse, that's my school and my town up there :-P I legitimately did a double take when I saw you."*

Nikki: *"Lol"*

Nikki: *"why cause I'm so pretty!"*

Dubbsy: *"umm yeaahhhh, you're so smart :-P Beauty and Brains, if only you didn't live in the stix."*

Nikki: *"There is plenty to do in XX."*

Dubbsy: *"Watching the numbers change at the Mcdonald's sign doesn't have the same affect on us city folk. :-P"*

Nikki: *"Whatever jerk, we know how to party! I gotta run tho, maybe I'll see you out this weekend."*

Dubbsy: *"Yeah maybe, later Nik."*

(I did not see her/text her that weekend, but she hit me up during the week)

Nikki: *"So I didn't see you stalking me this weekend, are you ok??"*

Dubbsy: *"Ahhh that means I did it the right way :-P you taught me well!"*

Nikki: *"Lol, you didn't go out to XX this weekend?"*

Dubbsy: "No I was away, last minute thing, how was it?"

Nikki: "It was XX same as usual."

Dubbsy: "Taking pictures of strangers to stalk later, a couple drinks here and there huh :)"

Nikki: "Ha! No!"

Dubbsy: "This isn't my first Rodeo Nik :-P"

Nikki: "Lol, do the jokes ever stop with you?"

Dubbsy: "Knock Knock."

Nikki: "Lol who's there?"

Dubbsy: "No."

Nikki: "haha. I get it."

Dubbsy: "there's only two reasons you'd laugh at that, 1) because it's the first joke you ever heard, or 2) because you have the lamest sense of humor ever :-P"

Nikki: "Lmao! You're ridiculous!! And I didn't laugh at that, it was a pity "haha"."

Dubbsy: "uhhh huh!! I gotta run tho, I'm definitely going to XX bar this weekend, it's my friends bday so we have the stage area reserved.. come thru and I'll see what I can do to get some small town girl and her friends in."

Nikki: "That would be awesome! We are def in."

Dubbsy: "Ok, I'll hit you up around then, if not by Saturday then remind me with a text, not a brick thru the window with a note (stalker style) :-P"

Nikki: "Lol ok jerk. See you Saturday!"

> **SOMETHING TO CONSIDER**
>
> If you find that you are constantly beginning in the Long Fuse phase, this could be a sign that you are making mistakes well before you get her phone number. If this is the case, then spend more time at the initial meet up mastering the steps outlined in Magic Bullets and see if that increases your success.

Long Fuse Strategies

Remember, while we do have strategies for burning down Long Fuses, the probability of converting these numbers is low. We suggest you attempt these simply for practice. We will try to burn down the occasional Long Fuse, but for the most part with forget about these numbers and move on.

The overall strategy for Long Fuses you meet through cold approach is to eventually turn them into Medium Fuses and/or Short Fuses. The strategies that can be employed to convert Long Fuses to Medium and Short Fuses are described below. Remember, these are focused on women you meet through cold approach. If the woman is a Long Fuse you will consistently see in your social circle, you will want to burn her down to a Medium Fuse or a Short Fuse in person before worrying about doing much on the phone.

Pinging and Keeping on Her Radar

A great strategy to implement with a Long Fuse is to stay on her radar by 'pinging'. Pinging is explored in depth in Chapter 6, however, in summary it involves sending the occasional low investment text message which is either funny or demonstrates value. These texts are sent on a random basis but there is usually at least a couple of days between each text message. While it is ok to ask questions, we suggest that you make at least half of them statements. When and if she replies, you do not go for the date. You simply mirror her level of investment, maybe asking for slightly more. Also, remember to end the interaction first if possible to help create tempo. This can be hard with Long Fuses, but when and if you get the chance, take it.

Good texts that you can use to ping with include:

"I just met your twin."

"Did you know that the blue whales tongue weighs more than an elephant? Gotta love national geographic."

"Hey I just wanted to touch base in case you get rich" (Source: THE ATTRACTION FORUMS)

"Remember guys tomorrow is 'Hug a retard' day. . . So don't freak out like you did last year, NO ONE IS TRYING TO HURT YOU!" (Source: THE ATTRACTION FORUMS)

"Brownies or fudge cake?"

"Pepperoni or Hawaiian?"

"Plane is about to take off... are you suppose to put your hands in the air like on a roller coaster?"

"You never write, you never call, rent is due, and the kids are worried sick. What should I tell them?"

"Hi Sara. Just thinking of you and wanted to say hi."

When she responds, keep flirting by teasing her but keep sexual overtones to a minimum until you gain more investment and comfort. The aim is to avoid becoming the 'creepy guy' that she kind of knows that always texts her. What you want to be instead is the cool guy who randomly makes her laugh and have fun. You are basically hanging around reminding her you are alive until the conditions in her life permit her to be a Medium Fuse or a Short Fuse again.

A Covert Tactic - the Mass Text

This tactic is basically another ping you can use. It involves texting her what seems to be a mass text to a bunch of people inviting her to something cool. Be sure to make it a group event. For example:

'My friends and I are doing X, grab your friends and stop by."

"Hey everyone... don't forget Kev's bday = our house tonight.

Swim suits = optional... arm floaties = Required...Safety first ;)."

"Hey all, Mike's farewell party at X Friday night. Your mission if you choose to accept it is to show up between the hours of 11pm and 2am. This message will self destruct in 30 sec! Hope to see you there...."

You can demonstrate value in this text by inviting her and her friends somewhere cool and exclusive (even if she does not come, she will mentally associate you with the venue or activity). She will also notice that you flirt with her every now and then, but you do not get creepy or pushy. However, do not send this text out too often or it may seem as if you are constantly asking people in your phone to come via mass text message instead of having strong personal relationships. Only use one fake mass text message every few weeks.

Do Not Seem Too Excited

A good rule of thumb is to double the time that you think that you should take between each call or text message. While you lose some text momentum by taking your time to reply, you also gain by credibly signaling non-neediness and abundance. Therefore, in general, for a Long Fuse, take your time in replying and vary the time that you take between replies to her text messages.

Do Not Get Emotional

> When dealing with a Long Fuse be patiently persistent.

It is also important never to be emotional when dealing with Long Fuses (or indeed with Short or Medium Fuses). Long Fuses are likely to flake, not reply, give short (almost rude) answers, etc. The mindset that you should have in these situations is that her actions have no bearing on your mood, because she is not yet important enough to you to commit any emotional energy to her. tions have no bearing on your mood, because she is not yet important enough to you to commit any emotional energy to her.

Take the following text exchange between Mr M and a Long Fuse called Heather as an example:

Heather: *(45 minutes later) "No more drinking for a couple of days.... back to work. Last night was FUN."*

Mr M: *(20 minutes later)* *"Must have been. You drunk txt me and tried to smooth talk me into coming to Movida. Lucky I'm a moral rock."*

Heather: *(10 minutes later)* *"Yeah right. Anyway I believe in no sex before marriage."*

Mr M: *(5 minutes later)* *"Whatever. And I dedicated my life to building orphanages for puppies that cannot bark. Don't make excuses because you're bad in bed."*

Heather: *(10 minutes later)* *"Well you'll never know honey."*

At this point, Mr M could react poorly and take this personally. Instead, he continues to have fun and tease her.

Mr M: *(10 minutes later)* *"Phew! I guess I get to stay a virgin for longer."*

Heather: *(12 hours later)* *"Lucky you."*

At this point, Mr M simply does not reply. He had nothing creative, fun or positive to say in response to her last text message so he instead chose not to say anything. However, he did not lash out and he did not lose value by trying to pander to her. It is not surprising then that 2 days later, she re engages him!

Heather: *(2 days later)* *"Talk to me :)"*

Have a Number of Long Fuses in Play

Ideally, you should have a number of fuses going on at once and not be dependent on any one Long or Medium Fuse. Keeping a number of Long Fuses going is a particularly good idea because you never know when the Long Fuse is going to go 'live' and turn into a Medium or Short Fuse.

This unpredictability is due to the fact that you do not know what is going on in a woman's life. Events may have occurred which are beyond your control which makes her turn from a Long to Medium or even Short Fuse (such as breaking up with a boyfriend). Moreover, having a number of Long Fuses going at once aligns your behaviors towards abundance because the loss of one Long Fuse will have no significant effect on you.

TIP: While it is ok to tease and flirt with a Long Fuse, it is important to calibrate as a Long Fuse will be the least forgiving of your mistakes. Therefore, when flirting with a Long Fuse, be mindful of her comfort threshold and investment limits and stay well within them. The more you practice the better and better you will get at this.

Be Patiently Persistent

A Long Fuse may take anywhere between a week to a year to convert. The key is to always stay on her radar and be patiently persistent so that you are there when her circumstances change. Usually what happens is you keep pinging with the same type of material and out of nowhere she is really receptive one day. Now you know you have a Medium Fuse and can begin treating her as such. When dealing with Long Fuses, you need to have a memory like a gold fish. This means you look at each text message as if it is the first one you have sent. You do not let your feelings get hurt from the past blow offs and you do not acknowledge them if and when she does finally come around.

<u>Long Fuse Example (by Braddock, Love Systems Instructor)</u>

I met Kelly through a cold approach. I teased her a little bit calling her Kelly Clarkson from American Idle. She was a number I took after a decent attraction set. I did not get to build much qualification or comfort. I did nothing wrong, she just became non responsive. I decided to text her once every few weeks just to see if I could get her to pop back up on the radar. She popped back up on one of my ping texts and we ended up hooking up. Turns out, when I first met her she had a boyfriend she was on the fritz with. They went out for a few more months and she has a rule that she doesn't flirt with/text/call boys when she has a boyfriend. However, they broke up after a few months and because I was always light and cool with my pings, she was receptive to a random text one night.

(Night we met)

Braddock: *"Nice meeting you tonight Kelly Clarkson... –Braddock."*

Kelly: *"lol... You too Oklahoma boy. Goodnight J."*

(Next Day. Sunday Evening):

Braddock: *"Hi rockstar....how is your Sunday?"*

Kelly: *(Nothing)*

(2 Days Later: (Call....no answer and no callback)

(3 Days Later)

Braddock: *"Traffic in LA is BRUTAL....I need a helicopter. ;)"*

Kelly: *(Nothing)*

(1 Week Later)

Braddock: *"Bunch of us going to Coco Deville tonight...you should stop by American Idol -Braddock."*

Kelly: *(Nothing)*

(2 Weeks Later: Send a fake mass text)

Braddock: *"Hey everyone...Don't forget Kev's bday = our house tonight.....Swim suits = optional...Arm floaties = Required...
Safety first ;)."*

Kelly: *(Nothing)*

(2 Weeks Later: Send a funny message....She FINALLY takes the bait)

Braddock: *"Plane is about to take off.....Are you suppose to put your hands in the air like on a roller coaster?"*

Kelly: *"hahaha....You are crazy Oklahoma! How have you been?"*

Braddock: *"American Idol......I thought maybe you joined the peace corp or some weird cult. :) How's your week?"*

Kelly 6:29pm: *"ha...No I didn't...Long story...We're goin out tonight. What are you doing?"*

(Now she is finally starting to act like a Medium Fuse. The worst thing I could do is start acting needy or chasing to hard. I want to have a memory like a gold fish and simply start texting her just like I would any other Medium Fuse. I happened to legitimately be going out of town. If I had been in town I would likely have grabbed a few of
my friends and capitalized on the invite).

> **Braddock 6:30pm:** "Wish I could…Sitting on a plane bout to take off for Miami sucka! ;)"
>
> **Kelly 6:31pm:** "Why didn't u take me with u?"
>
> **Braddock:** "You wouldn't like Miami anyway Kelly Clarkson…it's freezing there and the water is this ugly brown color…"
>
> **Kelly 6:34pm:** "lolol whatever….Why r u headed to Miami?"
>
> **Braddock:** "Teaching a workshop there."
>
> **Kelly 6:38pm:** "What's ur job? I'm jealous."
>
> **Braddock:** "I teach a self help seminar."
>
> **Kelly 6:39pm:** Serious?
>
> **Braddock:** "As a heart attack. :)"
>
> **Kelly 6:41pm:** "Wow! I want that job. Take me next time?"
>
> **Braddock:** "Deal….you're like 3 feet tall…you could easily fit in the carry on."
>
> **Kelly:** "lolol…I'm not that short jerk!"
>
> **Braddock:** "Alright…plane is taking off. Have fun tonight. Talk soon."
>
> **Kelly:** "Bye! Have a safe trip."

(Now I know we have a medium fuse because on the next day she texts me first…..and it's late at night. This means she is thinking about me. It was key that I did not initiate right away on the next day. I needed to create tempo and I needed to test and see if I have any tempo. If she had not sent the first text, I would have waited until another full day and then text her just to grab up emotional momentum. Tempo is best, but I'll take emotional momentum as a consolation prize if I have to).

Kelly 1:15am: *"When do u get back Oklahoma?"*

Braddock: *"Here til Monday...what's going on in LA tonight?"*

Kelly: *"Went to X bar...Pretty boring night. You aren't missing much."*

Braddock : *"Yeah Miami is pretty lame to.. with it's beach front bars.. and perfect weather. Who likes that crap? ;)"*

Kelly: *"LoL...Now you are being mean.... I'm off to bed. Don't have to much fun in Miami babe"*

(The Next Monday)

Braddock: *"Arts Festival this week + Funnel Cakes = Braddock eats 20+ and gets sick."*

Kelly12:42pm: *"haha..I love the Arts Festival! I don't get to go...I wish I could come with you...I have to work :"*

(That was me attempting to bait her. I wanted to take the temperature and see where she stood. Remember, this girl wouldn't even reply to a text a few weeks ago. I do not want to spook her off by moving to fast. She is now a medium fuse. If I push to fast I could make her a long fuse just like that).

Braddock: *"Poor Kelly. I wouldn't miss funnel cakes for a close friends funeral."*

Kelly: *"haha....I know! This sucks!!!"*

(Next Day)

Braddock: *"I'm going on another business trip this weekend....You still down for riding carry on?"*

Kelly 2:30pm: *"haha..Heck yes ill go! I love flying...Where to this time!?"*

Braddock: "Don't lie…you've never flown…Flights have a height requirement just like amusement parks… "You have to be this tall to ride the ride"….Chicago."

Kelly 10:25am: "Haha shut it! I'm 5'5" with heels mr. I wish I traveled as much as u."

(We text back and forth for another week. She works harder to answer my questions and plays along with role plays. She also initiates quite a few of the interactions. Because of this, she is now a short fuse and I decide to go for the meet up.)

Braddock 7:44pm: "Kelly Kapowski wanna grab a drink tonight?"

Kelly 7:53pm: "Sure! What time? Nice Saved by The Bell reference by the way…lol."

Braddock 7:58pm: "Sweeet! I'm actually in New York. If you can leave 5 hours ago, you can make it on time :)"

Kelly 8:09pm: "hahahahaha! Who does that jerk!?"

Braddock: "LoL….Home tomorrow, drink then? ;)"

Kelly: "lol…You are crazy. Sounds good. Ill see you tomorrow pimp."

(Met up and went on a date and hooked up that night. This is amazing considering the amount of obstacles I had to deal with. Just remember, that many times they are dealing with other things in their life, they were actually dating someone when you took the number, or they start dating someone a few weeks into talking to you. Just hang in there. Fade out, but hang in there. Do not leak emotionally and do not force her to say no by putting pressure on her. Make it easy for her to say "yes" down the road.)

Key Points of this Chapter

- Short Fuses are characterized by high levels of investment and it is typically not difficult to turn a Short Fuse into a date. The key strategy for a Short Fuse is simply, 'do not mess it up'.

- Go for a date with a Short Fuse. Not acting on a Short Fuse can lead to her turning into a Medium or Long Fuse.

- Avoid spending too much time on the phone with a Short Fuse until you have seen her again in person. You do not want to risk turning a Short Fuse into Long Fuse. The key is to get her out on a date with you and escalate in person.

- There are two central strategies that you can use to turn a Medium Fuse into a Short Fuse:
 (1) Extend a "you guys should meet us out" invitation
 (2) Continue to text and ping her over time and build attraction by displaying humor, value and non-neediness.

- The overall strategy for Long Fuses is to eventually turn them into Medium and/or Short Fuses.

- Stay on a Long Fuse's radar by pinging her and inviting her and her friends out to group events.

- Have multiple Long Fuses going on at once. Never depend on any one Long or Medium Fuse.

CHAPTER 6 – FURTHER TEXT AND PHONE GAME TACTICS

IN THIS CHAPTER:

- The Ideal Days and Times to Text
- Pinging
- Baiting
- Playing Roles
- Messages For Short or Medium Fuses on Pause
- Pull Back On The Reins
- Leaving Voicemails

Chapter 6 – Further Text and Phone Game Tactics

This chapter explores powerful Text and Phone Game strategies and tactics. Although it may take some time for you to learn to properly use some of these tactics (particularly the more advanced ones), when you do implement them correctly, they will have a very profound effect on your Text and Phone Game.

The Ideal Days to Text

Texting an attractive woman on a Friday or Saturday night when most people are usually out enjoying a good time is not ideal (unless you know where she is and are trying to meet her out). A better time to text is usually in the afternoon or evening outside of these days. Sunday evening in particular is good. For most people Sunday evening is usually characterized by a relaxing time alone at home. It is in this situation that she is more likely to respond to your text messages.

A Note on Ending Conversations First

There is no need to end conversations first when things are going very well. You should use this time to gain momentum and investment.

However, when you can feel that the 'high note' is about to be reached (i.e. the conversation can only go down from this point as it is on such a high), then be the first one to either end the conversation or simply stop replying.

This may sound counter-intuitive, but it is a key step in winning the 'Tempo' war and gaining investment.

The Ideal Time to Text

The ideal time to text is usually after she has had dinner and before she sleeps. If she keeps a normal job, this will generally be between the hours of 8pm and 11pm. If you text around these hours, it is likely that you will be the last person she thinks about before she goes to sleep. This can have a powerful effect on her emotional attachment to you. Feel free to use your ping texts almost anytime during the day.

Pinging

Pinging is the art of keeping yourself on a woman's radar in between meet ups or while you are trying to get her from a Long to Short Fuse. Pinging helps to fill in the gaps between seeing her and even between your phonecalls. Even if the first interaction was very strong and she is a Short Fuse, there may be a period of time before you get to meet her again where you should maintain contact with her and 'ping'. If you are not pinging a woman, by the time that you get around to meeting her she may have forgotten what was so great about you that made her want to meet up with you in the first place. This can lead to her flaking.

The way to ping a woman between meet ups is to text her short and humorous thoughts that do not warrant a phone call, but create a fun and playful vibe between the two of you. The texts should not be overtly sexual, nor should they be overly kiss ass messages (although you can introduce racier messages if you are baiting her). Ideally, pinging text messages should lead to her laughing or smiling.

Here are some examples of pinging texts which can be sent between meet ups:

> ***Braddock:*** *"After careful consideration, I have come to the conclusion that everyone in this Airport sucks except me. Tell your friends."*
>
> ***Braddock:*** *"Nobu = best restaurant ever... just below Taco Bell. Why would anyone choose to use chop sticks? I would starve to death if I had to use these all the time."*
>
> ***Braddock:*** *"Tequila 4. Braddock 0. I would kill a small child for a Tylenol."*
>
> ***Braddock:*** *"Us not talking for 2 months is going beyond playing hard to get. You're going to drive me into the arms of several other women at this rate."*
>
> ***Braddock:*** *"We need to talk. . . . I'm pretty sure I'm pregnant."*
>
> ***Braddock:*** *"Just wanted to remind everyone that I'm cooler than the other side of the pillow. Tell your friends."*

Braddock: *"Hey, I met this really cute girl form (city) last night, what should I say to flirt with her?"*

Braddock: *"Wow…walking to my car, some old lady just tole me I'm bootylicious. Awesome….I think."*

Braddock: *"If Santa was real, he'd be locked away for being a pedophile…We basically celebrate pedophilia every December..kinda messed up. We'll let a creepy old man in our house for gifts…pretty sad!"*

Braddock: *"Tiger Woods asked Santa not 4 a white Christmas, but for another white mistress."*

Braddock: *"Just watched that movie 300…Awesome! Don't remember them shooting that documentary of my life, but that's cool."*

Braddock: *"Jersey Shore = Best show ever! So trashy…but can't stop watching it."*

Daxx: *"Traffic in LA makes mowing your lawn with scissors seem fun. I need a helicopter."*

Here is an example of an interaction, which eventuated from a 'ping':

Braddock: *"Echo 1 this is Bravo Company…kksssh. Nip/Tuck in t-minus 5 min…. kkshh. I repeat: mother bird is in her nest…. kkshh. Repeat: the crips are raiding the liquor store. Copy? Over…."*

Linda B: *"Bravo company this is Echo one and I'm pickin up what you're putting down but unfortunately I won't be privy to such luxuries as nip tuck, tonight bc I have other engagements to tend to…"*

Linda B: *"such as studying for exams and preparing for my interview tomorrow morning…I'm counting on you to take notes and provide a detailed summary of the nights events. Think you can handle that?... Kkshh…Over…"*

Braddock: *"Roger that Lima Bravo. That's a 10-28 (loud & clear). Tango X Ray will be in service. Zulu acknowledges message & will return to headquarters w/assignment completed."*

Braddock: *"Delta Foxtrot has Tivo ready & waiting for mission. Report by landline after your tasks are completed b/c Romeo Delta wants a full debriefing of enemy engagements. Divide & conquer all tasks this week. Hoo-rah!"*

Linda B: *"LoLoLoLoL"*

Pinging multiple times can have very powerful effects:

> 1. Pinging allows you to look non needy while still keeping in contact with her (i.e. staying on her radar).
> 2. Pinging builds comfort and investment, particularly if she re sponds and this leads to a text conversation.
> 3. Pinging can build attraction if you are making her laugh with your text messages.
> 4. Pinging can reveal if she is ready to go from a Long Fuse to a Medium Fuse or a Medium Fuse to a Short Fuse based on her response to your ping.

Baiting

Baiting is how you gradually escalate all facets of text and phone game including: teasing, building comfort, going for the meet, and sexualizing. Baiting keeps you from making bold moves and allows you to take calculated risks. Baiting is throwing out very subtle flirtatious jokes, innuendos, invites, misinterpretations or comments to see if she 'bites' or not.

If she 'takes the bait', meaning she responds positively or at least neutral, you now have access to dialogue that was not previously available. If she responds positively to the bait, you can now push the envelope in that area. If she does not take the bait, ignores it completely or reacts negatively, you should not escalate things any farther in that area yet. If you are baiting properly you should lose no value or investment on the times when she does not take the bait because you should be doing them incrementally.

Remember, the shorter the fuse, the less baiting you will need. If it is a Short Fuse, you still have the option of baiting, but being more transparent about your intentions is usually fine.

Examples of baiting to meet up (discussed in depth in Chapter 9) are:

- [Reply to her previous text] Braddock: "If we don't hang out soon then I'm going to start cheating on you. :)" [Note that this is text message also baits for Sexualization through implementing a cheating/marriage/relationship role play].

Or..

- [Reply to her previous text] Braddock: "Tell your interns to pencil me in for next week or I'm putting 'single' back up on facebook."

Examples of baiting for Sexualization (discussed in depth in Chapter 8) include:

Her: "I'm at home, pretty sick... in bed..."

Mr M: "Boo. Did I give you that cough? I tried to tell you no making out but you wouldn't listen. Next time, no means no, or I call the cops."

Remember that baiting is not taking a high investment shot in the dark and hoping that she will go for it. Baiting, when executed properly, should hint at or assume only slightly more investment than you already have from her to see if she is going to allow you to go there yet or not. In fact, early baiting is so subtle that she should almost not notice the temperature change. If things were going great and the goes cold after you attempted to bait, it is likely that you baited to far for her investment level.

Playing Roles

Playing roles is an advanced but important concept in Text and Phone Game. Playing roles is first and foremost about being aware of what frame and personality you put across to the woman in your initial interaction. Once you are aware of that frame or personality, it is important that you either (a) maintain it over text and phone or (b) understand what can happen if you decide to change it.

Here are some examples of the different sides of yourself (or roles) that you could put across to the woman in your initial interaction:

1. The classy guy.
2. The guy who was shamelessly attracted to her.
3. The sweet guy who plays it safe and goes for getting the date.

4. The sexual guy (heavy on the sexual talk, framing and sexual vibe).
5. The booty call (friends with benefits).
6. The asshole guy (heavy on the cocky funny and smart ass comments).
7. The high value guy who she should get to know and hang out with.

Before you initiate Text and Phone Game with a woman, think about what role she sees you as having in her life based on your first interaction. Ask yourself – "what role did I play in the first encounter, even if it was unintentional?" Roles can be frustrating because sometimes you can get stuck in a role you did not mean to play. Maybe you met her in a situation where it was hard to assert your personality so you ended up looking shy even though you are quite fun and outgoing around your normal friends. Roles can help you as well. If you were shamelessly attracted to her when you met, then you will be able to carry on this role through text and phone. Transitioning to the 'sexual guy' will not be as hard, compared to if you were the 'shy guy' when you met.

If you played the 'classy guy' when you met, it will come across strange if you do a 180 degree turn and start playing the role of the 'sexual guy.' If you played the 'asshole guy' role, then it will feel strange to her if you switch gears immediately to 'sweet guy'.

You can change roles. However, you need to make the change gradual and use baiting to test
(a) whether she is comfortable with you switching roles and
(b) how fast you can make the switch. For example, you could meet a woman in a situation where it would be socially uncalibrated to talk sexual, but when you start texting or calling, the window to take things sexual can open quickly. In this case, you can use baiting to switch roles.

If you choose to disregard the role a woman has for you, you are essentially throwing darts blind folded and hoping that they hit. A woman may be the type to give a Short Fuse to the 'classy guy' but give a Medium or Long Fuse to the 'sexual man'. In that example, if you had role played 'classy guy' in your initial encounter and you suddenly switched to 'sexual man' over text, you would be making the situation much more difficult.

Really pay attention to your roles. Do not play a weak role in person and hope that this book will have lines you can cut and paste to fix your poor performance in person. A weak role in person will create massive problems with your phone and text game.

Messages For Short or Medium Fuses on Pause

Sometimes women fall off the map for a few weeks or months even though they are interested and you did nothing wrong. Often times the woman did not become a Long Fuse, she was simply busy. Her investment level is unchanged. These messages are only useful for women who were very Short or Medium Fuses at one point (i.e. you could tell that they were very into you), but for some reason, lost momentum and interest.

These messages are a non needy way to remind her that you are still interested. They should asks a non needy, real question which is tempered by humor. The humor element is important so that the woman does not sense weakness or bitterness, but at the same time she can tell that you are serious. You should ensure that a fair amount of time has passed (perhaps a week or more) before sending a takeaway message. The danger of sending a takeaway message too soon is that it could appear as if it is a desperate response to her investment dropping.

Here is an example:

> ***Braddock:*** *"What up [insert Callback Humor nickname]? Are we breaking up for real this time?"*

Or..

> ***Braddock:*** *"I miss your face! What have you been up to kiddo?"*

Or..

> ***Braddock:*** *"There is this really cute girl from Boston that I used to flirt with...but I think she got kidnapped. Thinking about sending a search party."*

Or..

> ***Braddock:*** *"There is this really cute girl named Kathy that I really want to see, but she is sooo flaky...Any suggestions on making a date happen? (I won't tell her you told me)"*

Or...

Braddock: *"You never write…you never call…rents due…and the kids are worried sick. What should I tell them?"*

Or..

Braddock: *"Miss talking to you Missouri…"*

Or..

Braddock: *"I'm officially changing my facebook and seeing other people you this week if I don't hear from you!"*

Or..

Braddock: *"Flirt with me…Readyyyyyyyy go! ;)"*

Or..

Braddock: *"(Insert something witty and charming that makes Angela grab a drink this week)"*

If she responds positively by saying something like "Where are you?" or "I want to see you", then flirt and tease hard and push for the meet up, but do not break the sexual tension by dropping everything immediately to go and see her. The key is to not come across as too excited or desperate to meet up, but instead to reminder her that you are still around and interested in flirting.

Pull Back On The Reins (Correcting Bad Behavior)

Stirring a woman emotionally is advanced and should be used as a last ditch tactic. It is particularly useful for when a good situation has started to go bad and/or if you think that it would help change her behavior towards you. It should not be used if things are moving along perfectly.

Stirring the woman emotionally will only work if you had high investment from the woman at one point in time. If she has not invested emotionally in the encounter, then this tactic will not have any effect and the woman will simply forget about you and not reply.

The ideal way to stir a woman emotionally is to change your behavior noticeably from the way you have behaved previously. So, whereas you have been playful and light the entire time, you can suddenly turn serious. The key is that she can tell that something has changed in you.

Importantly, the trigger for your change in behavior must be something that she says or does over text. It can be a text message that is either obviously open to misinterpretation or a text message which truly is on the rude side. However, it cannot be just any 'reasonable' response from her. Misinterpretation or rudeness generally must be involved.

Here are some ways to emotionally stir the woman. These can be used by themselves or in combination if the situation allows:

> 1. Saying something rude after her last text and then going ra dio silence.
> 2. Giving her a one word or short response that's cold and shows you do not care what she thinks anymore:
> a. "Right"
> b. "Fuck it"
> c. "Whatever"
> d. "Sure."
> 3. Stop replying to her texts until she calls and explains her last message.
> 4. Send a short business like text calling her out on her rude behavior, but be extremely vague. Then stop replying to her texts until she calls you.
> 5. Same as (2), but reply only after she has sent multiple texts explaining herself. In doing so, you still wait a while (30 minutes to an hour) to reply, and even then your replies are short and pointed.
> 6. Be abrupt with your responses and take much longer than usual to reply. Only let your guard down after she apologizes, and explains how she didn't mean it.

Be careful not to overdo the business like behavior. If you try to hold a 'hard front' for too long, her ego will eventually kick in and she will revert back to being rude. If that happens, it is almost impossible to recover. Instead, cycle between business like texts and light texts.

The main aim of stirring a woman emotionally is not to 'punish' her, but to change the temperature of the interaction. This demonstrates several positive things which include your ability to walk away from the woman if she does not live up to your standards and expectations, that you have strong boundaries that you will enforce and that you only show the stern side of yourself when you must (i.e. you effectively demonstrate that you are a man who prefers to be fun and light but are serious if you need to be, which is very powerful).

Voicemail

If you call her and the phone does not ring, but goes directly to voicemail, hang up. There will be no missed call on her phone and she will not know that you called.
However, if the phone rings and you get her voicemail, either she did not get to her phone in time or she saw your number and did not feel like talking to you at that moment. In this situation, it is best to leave her a 'call-to-action message'. You want her to return the call and one way to do this is to leave a message which involves an open loop.

Examples of this include:

- "I didn't know you knew my friend Kelly… [hang up]"
- "My friend said that you… [hang up on yourself]"
- "Oh my god, you'll never guess what just happened… [hang up]"

Note that these may be preceded by a description of something that was relevant to her (for example, a story) or callback humour. The key is to pick something that is true and that you can be congruent with, but to remember to leave the open loop by hanging up.

An alternative option is to leave a humorous message. These messages usually work best on Short or Medium Fuses with whom you have played a role which involves you teasing her and being funny. The reason that this is important is that although the message may be funny, it is important that it is congruent with your personality. If you have been the serious guy all along and suddenly leave a very humorous voicemail, she may think that it seems out of character for you and confuse her. Be sure to calibrate the use of humorous messages – particularly the ones given as examples below:

- ***Braddock:*** *"Hi. I found this number on the bathroom at [nearest sta-*

tion]. It said call [her name] for a good time. My name is [your name] and I am up for a good time so if you could call me on [your number] maybe we can meet up."

• **Braddock:** *"Hi. This is [your name] from WalMart. I'm just calling you to thank you for your application for the job of check out chick and to inform you that you didn't get the job... I'm afraid that you are not qualified to work as a check out chick but please don't be discouraged. I think Aldo down the road are looking for a cleaner and they might accept you there. Thanks."*

• **Braddock:** *"Hi. This is the manager down here at Christy's Toy box [or whatever sex toys store near you]. Listen, I know you are a platinum member, but this is your 3rd bounced check this week. I'm going to need you to come down here and take care of this today or we are cutting of your credit line down here at the store. You can call me back at XXX-XXXX."*

Key Points of this Chapter

- Initiate conversation using low investment text messages.

- Ping a woman between meet ups by texting her short and humorous thoughts that do not warrant a phone call. Use these texts to create and maintain a fun and playful vibe between the two of you.

- Bait her by throwing out very subtle flirtatious jokes, innuendos, invites, misinterpretations or comments to see if she 'bites' or not.

- Ask yourself "what role did I play during the first encounter?" You can change roles, but make the change gradual and use baiting to test whether she is comfortable with you switching and how fast you can make that switch.

- Takeaway messages can be used for woman who were Short Fuses at one point, but for some reason lost momentum and interest.

- Stirring a woman emotionally is an advanced tactic which can be used when a good situation has started to go bad.

- If you call her and get her voicemail, it is best to leave a 'call to action message'.

CHAPTER 7 - BUILDING VALUE AND GENERATING ATTRACTION

IN THIS CHAPTER:

- Using the Eight Attraction Triggers
- Told Versus Observed
- Tempo
- Manipulating Tempo
- Frame Setting
- Getting Her to Take Positive Action
- More Text Message Attraction Strategies
- Qualification over Text Message

Chapter 7 - Building Value and Generating Attraction

Using the Eight Attraction Triggers

As described in , there are eight main attraction triggers:

- Health
- Social Intuition
- Humor
- Status
- Wealth
- Confidence
- Pre-selection
- Challenge

These triggers can be conveyed through Text and Phone Game to create value and attraction. In this chapter, we will investigate how.

Told Versus Observed

An important distinction to make when demonstrating value is between a told and observed conveyance. For example, imagine that you are trying to convey the attraction trigger of 'health'. There are two main ways in which you could do this:

1) TOLD EXAMPLE (NOT IDEAL):

"I'm really good at 5 different types of sports"
"I keep social, fit and healthy all the time"

2) OBSERVED EXAMPLE (IDEAL):

After having a short text exchange: "Cool. I'm off to the gym. Too much texting = big fingers small guns. Spk soon x"

After having a short text exchange: "We should catch up. I'm playing soccer right now so I can only hang out after 8"

In the above example, both the 'told' and 'observed' methods attempt to convey the same attraction trigger – that you are a healthy and active individual. However, the observed form is far more effective. A key principle in Text and Phone Game is that the attraction trigger must be conveyed in such a way that it is either:

(a) secondary to, or a byproduct of, the subject matter of the text or phone call,
(b) disguised by humor or
(c) subtly woven into the subject matter.

Note too that the line – "Cool. I'm off to the gym. Too much texting = big fingers small guns. Spk soon x" will not immediately create attraction or value on its own. While it is possible to generate attraction extremely quickly through text message using techniques like Callback Humor, other attraction triggers are more difficult and slower to communicate via text. Consequently, it is the cumulative build up of various attraction triggers, through personality conveying texts (such as the health ones above) that will paint the picture in her mind of an attractive man over time. Ideally, you would have a mix of buying temperature attraction (through using attraction triggers such as humor) and high value attraction (through using attraction triggers such as health and status). If you do not understand the difference between the different types of attraction, see Mr M's highly acclaimed article on the different types of attraction here.

Examples of Texts for Each Attraction Trigger

Below are some examples of texts that can be used to hit attraction triggers. The way that you communicate these attraction triggers over the phone is not dissimilar to how you would communicate them in-field. This is described in detail in. In this section, the main focus will be communicating attraction triggers over text message. Note that certain attraction triggers are more suited to effective demonstration in person rather than over text message. For example, the attraction triggers of, health, status and wealth and pre-selection can be more powerfully demonstrated when you are with her, rather than over text.

Health
Health is typically most effectively demonstrated in person. However, it

can be conveyed through text, mostly through conveying an active life. Examples include:

> **After having a short text exchange:** "Cool. I've got a game to get to. Too much texting = carpel tunnel syndrome. Spk soon x"

> **After she asks you what you are doing:** "Playing flag football. We need a mascot… put on a duck costume and get down here dork ;)"

A good idea is to mix the fact that you are doing an activity with humor or Callback Humor (such as in the second text message above).

Social Intuition

Social intuition is most easily communicated via text by good teasing, joking and playful banter. For an example, see the below text exchange. The background is that the woman just came back from a holiday in Paris.

> *Mr M: "Comment ca va stalker? Did you bring presents from Paris?"*
>
> *Her: "Well I got u a beret and a string of onions u like?"*
>
> *Mr M: "You know me so well! Its times like this that keep me coming back to you even though you hit me and the sex is bad."*
>
> *Her: "Ha ha well sometimes a beating is what u needed… how many times did I have to tell u to put the toilet seat down! And the sex…well… I was faking it."*
>
> *Mr M: "Fake my ass. You were so loud you woke the neighbors up. Can you FedEx me the onions and beret so I don't have to see you again please…we are breaking up."*

Note the high level of teasing and banter which edges on social inappropriateness, but does not go over. The fact that Mr M is able to banter with her so well on such a socially taboo but fun role play indicates that he has a high level of social intuition, which is attractive.

Alternatively, social intuition can be more directly demonstrated by displaying social alliances and social dominance. For example:

Her: "What are you up to?"

Mr M: "Out partying with [name of two good high value friends] and a donkey..."

Or

Her: "What did you do last night?"

Mr M: "Went to see [name of band] with [name of high value friend].. got to hang out backstage! It was awesome sauce."

Notice that Mr M combines the mention of value with humor or Callback Humor (in the above examples mentioning a 'donkey' for humor and using the Callback Humor 'awesome sauce'). Humor can be used to take away the 'edge' from the value spike and decreases the chance that she will perceive you to be simply bragging.

Humor

At this point in the book we have showed multiple ways you can use humor and discussed in great detail the importance of humor. There are a number of different ways to use humor. The best type of humor to use for text message we have already discussed ant that is Callback Humor and role plays. Humor is a great tool to generate attraction, be challenging, soften going for the meet up, soften sexualization, and every kind of baiting. Let's look at an example where Braddock uses different types of humor.

Braddock met Chantal while he was in Boston. She was a bartender and was working the night of his birthday. They have been talking off and on for several months now. Even though she was a Short Fuse for a long time, she fell off the map for a while because she lives in Boston and Braddock lives in Los Angeles. Eventually she got a boyfriend. Even though she had a boyfriend they would text and flirt a lot. Even though they do not get to see each other often and she has a boyfriend she stays attracted because he keeps a good banter and uses humor to keep things fun.

Braddock: "You back in the US jet setter?"

Chantal: "You missss me! Just got in today. It's 37 degrees, I'm psyched."

Braddock: *"Did you and your pops have a fun Christmas? Actually looking forward to the cold Boston winter, huh? South Africa that hot!?"*

Chantal: *"I guess my sarcasm doesn't read well over SMS...Had a great time with dad. Didn't want to leave at all. When are you back in LA?"*

Braddock: *"lol..fucking smart ass. I'll be back in LA in 5 hours. Plane is taking off in 10..sitting on it."*

Braddock: *"What are you doing for New Years Boston girl? Bible study like me?"*

Chantal: *"I'm thinking you and me in the biblical sense...I could think of worse ways to ring in the New Year."*

Braddock: *"You mean take our clothes off? Allll the way off? (Gulp of nervousness)"*

Chantal: *"lol...maybe not all the way off, I know you are REAL shy."*

Chantal: *"I have an interview with a customs agent in a minute...Let's hope those gloves aren't latex."*

Braddock: *"Tell her if she talks dirty or makes eye contact....it costs extra $100."*

Chantal: *"My price is $1,000. She knows that.."*

Braddock: *"That's a pretty good price considering we are in a recession."*

Chantal: *"Don't forget to get me a sweeet bday present."*

Braddock: *"What do you want? Microwave? Spatula? Optimus Prime toy? How about a nice hug..."*

Chantal: *"I'll take what I got you for your 26th...that was hot....or a pony."*

Braddock: *"Ooo..so I should be a rude bartender and give you one free shot and a bunch of smart ass comments?? Done."*

Chantal: *"LoLoL....whatever! You ended up getting something pretty damn good. Besides, you and your friends were retards, you deserved it. I had to get drunk to deal with you. :)"*

Braddock: *"I'm a drunk 7....at least."*

Chantal: *"I recently took up painting and mozaicing..If I remember you're quite the Jackon Pollock."*

(She has used this exact joke several months ago the night we met. I immediately tease her about recycling jokes).

Braddock: *" LOLOL..wow...are you recycling jokes on me Chantal?!? I expect you to have more game than that......you used the Jackson Pollok joke the first night I stayed with you!!"*

Braddock: *"How the mighty have fallen since getting a boyfriend.... It's nice of you to recycle though...very environmentally conscientious."*

Chantal: *"uh...whatever...green is in sucka."*

Chantal: *"and don't believe everything you read on facebook. I wouldn't have sent you that pic last week if I still had a BF."*

Braddock: *"Green is definitely in...that was Honda Hybrid Green."*

Chantal: *"God you are a dick! How did you even remember that?!"*

Braddock: *"Memory like an old elephant playa ;)."*

Braddock: *"Ok..plane is taking off. I'll recycle with you.. "hands up on take off like on a roller coaster?" (I've used that on her several times)*

Chantal: *"ugh..can't believe you remembered that...fucker."*

Braddock: *"Good luck with your customs date...I hope she's funny, rich, and has great abs."*

Chantal: *"lololol....fly safe. Call me when you land."*

In the absence of Callback Humor, there are great one-liners you can ping with such as:

"Hey. Do me a favor and text me right back. Just hi or something. My friends don't believe retards can text. We'll show em lil buddy"
(Source: THE ATTRACTION FORUMS)

"Aliens are coming to abduct all the sexy people off the planet and force them to breed. You should be safe, I just wanted to text to say goodbye."
(Source: THE ATTRACTION FORUMS)

The best way to get better with humor is to practice being funny, being around funny people and watching funny videos and movies. This applies to Text and Phone Game, you're in-field ability and also to general social situations. Review the section on Callback Humor in Chapter 2 for more on how to use and develop your 'humor muscles'.

Status and Wealth

Status and wealth are generally more difficult to display via text message. The main problem is that if done incorrectly, the conveyance of status and wealth is easily misconstrued as bragging. There are, however, certain 'sisters' to demonstrating wealth which can show status. A wealthy person is likely to have achieved excellence in what he does and have strong social alliances. You can easily convey these factors through text. For example:

Her: "How was your wkend?"

Mr M: "Awesome. Partied all weekend with buddies from Australia at [name of exclusive club]. p.s. Do you like Ben Harper?"

Her: "Yeh, I like some of their tracks. p.s. was one of them Steve Irwin lol…"

Mr M: "Crikey no but Crocodile Dundee was there lol. I just wrote a song that sounds like Ben Harper. Might perform it live next week."

In the above exchange, Mr M mentions quite a few facts subtly in order to build value. The first fact is that he has international friends who came to see him. This is both social proof and a demonstration of social alliances (one of the attraction triggers for social circle pick up, as covered in SOCIAL CIRCLE MASTERY). The second is that he parties and has a good time at some of the top clubs in his area, which is personality conveying and shows that he has a fun and interesting lifestyle. The third is that he writes music and is playing live. The fact that he plays live is evidence of status.

Note that you do not have to play live music to take advantage of the status attraction switch. Generally, anything that you do in a leadership role is something that you can mention to illustrate status. Examples may include making a speech, organizing a group, or leading a conference or team. Although the way you lead in your life will vary on a case by case basis for every reader, the principle remains the same – you can subtly show her that you have status by mentioning and/or describing a position of leadership.

One option you have for doing this is by talking about your friends instead of yourself. If your friends are cool and have cool lives, it is assumed that you are one of them. Another option here is to reward and relate to the cool things she talks about. If she says she loves London, you can reward and relate by saying, "London's great…but Prague is my favorite." This Shows high value traits without coming across like you are trying to impress her or bragging.

Confidence

It is hard to 'show confidence' in any one text. Confidence is typically conveyed very subtly through the overall tone of the text messaging. The general principles of conveying confidence through text are:

> 1. Do not use too many 'LOL's', 'haha' or smiley faces in texts to avoid seeming weak or emotionally overreaching.
> 2. Avoid long winded, comfort building texts.
> 3. Vary the time you take to reply to texts – do not always reply immediately and as a general rule, wait between
> 5 minutes and sometimes several hours.
> 4. Try to be the one to end the interaction on a high point.
> 5. Baiting and pushing the envelope using push/pull when the time is right.
> 6. Do not answer every question of her texts. Answer what you want and feel free to change the subject with out addressing every question.

Below is an example of a dialogue which shows confidence:

[When ending the interaction] ***Mr M:*** "OK, hitting the sack.... so I'm out. p.s. it's $40 p/hr for the funny texts. Let me know where I should send the bill...goodnight ;)"

Another Example

Mr M: "What up kaley/amy/billy hawthorn?" [Callback Humor]

Her: "What up Bruce! Hows it going ill check you on facebush next week x" [Callback Humor]

Mr M: "No you won't because I blocked you"

Her: "Ha Ha oh really yea am a bit of a stalker so maybe for the best ;) got no phone signal here!! Paris tomorrow ha ha woo! x"

Mr M: "Thanks for the invite to Paris, can't go this week some of us have to work. Ps that's not going to get you in my pants stalker. Gnight billy x"

As you can see, in the conversation above, Mr M shows a lot of confidence. He does not overuse LOL's or 'haha' and keeps replies varied but generally short. Moreover, he ends the conversation first instead of seeming needy. See the section on Tempo (below) for a more detailed look about how to show confidence.

Pre-selection

Pre-selection is best demonstrated in person or over the phone. If you are going to attempt pre selection through text it is best to allude to it and let her mind assume things. If you try to brag abou the hot girls you are with, you will look like a fool. However, pre selection can be conveyed via texts by saying things like:

> [In reply to her asking where you are] ***Braddock:*** "Hey sexy...I'm at my friend Sara's b day party at (hot club in your area)."
>
> [In reply to her asking where you are] ***Braddock:*** "I'm with my friend Katie and Jessica watching Avatar."
>
> [In reply to her asking what are you doing tonight] ***Braddock:***

> "My friend Jessica is modeling in a fashion show tonight and she asked us to come give some support. Should be done 9ish. What are you up to?"

Challenge

The best way to show Challenge is by not seeming too eager. There are a number of ways of achieving this and they are the topic of the section on Tempo, immediately below.

There are also some specific 'framing' texts which you can send to hit the Challenge attraction switch. These texts show that you are non-needy and trying to figure her out. They could be common qualifying questions that you only subtly reward or they could be texts that establish the frame (or the one who is slowly winning you over). Frame setting is covered later in this chapter.

Tempo

What Is Tempo?

A person has 'Tempo' in a text conversation if that person is controlling the emotional climate of the communication. To use an example to illustrate, have you ever experienced that sinking feeling when you send a text and do not receive one back in return for a while? You end up thinking about how stupid you were to send the text and incessantly wonder whether or not you have actually done anything wrong. You may even send a follow up text to make sure that she is OK with it. In this situation, the woman has Tempo. You are thinking more about her than she is about you. She is dictating the 'emotional climate'. The great thing is that Tempo can easily be manipulated and reversed.

Manipulating Tempo – Using The Law of Varying Returns

Varying both the time you take to reply, and the quality of your returns, can be devastatingly effective in getting a woman almost addicted to waiting for your next text. Your two major tools here are time to reply and length of text messages:

- Time to reply

    To win 'Tempo' and build attraction, you should vary the time and content of your replies.

    Sometimes it will be a good idea to reply immediately. However, other times, reply anywhere between 5 minutes to a couple of hours. This signifies that she is not the most important thing in your life and keeps her off balance. To use this even more powerfully, take your timereplying to her when she says something that could be misinter preted as strange, different or provoking. This is intended to make her recheck her message or think about why you have not responded. You know that this is to working when you get 'double texts' from her (i.e. she texts you twice over a period of time between texts before you text her back).

Two Basic Rules for Building Value and Gaining Tempo over Text

1) Avoid Sending More Than One Text in a Row

As a general rule, do not send two texts in a row. If you have to do this, then you should call the second time. It shows decisiveness. If she does not pick up, allow her to reengage or simply contact her again in a couple of days with a funny text message or call.

2) End the Conversation First At Least 80% of the Time

You should always try to be the one to end the conversation. This keeps you from looking like a needy guy while texting. Ending a conversation is easy. You simply say, after a text exchange, 'Anyway, I've got friends over [or some other distraction that gives you value], so I better go. Spk soon [nickname]' or simply don't reply to her last text.

- Length of text messages

    As a general principle, brevity is preferred in text messages. That being said, you can create strong attraction by varying the length of your text messages. For example, by replying to her texts with simple words such as 'OK' or 'sure' (for the affimative) or 'Not really' or 'Nope' (for the negative), you can reassert your non-needy frame or suggest your dislike for some aspect of her last text. This seems counter intuitive, but it is actually an effective signaling mechanism that she has not won you over completely yet. For example, this was a recent text message exchange that Mr. M had with a Playboy Playmate:

Playmate: *"Well, what do you suggest then, mister?"*

Mr M: *"I'm having drinks and playing twister at the hotel. Come play and we'll go from here."*

Playmate: *"I got work tomorrow – and I'm way too tired for anything tonight anyways – drinks tomorrow?"*

Mr M: *(after approx 25 minutes) "Sure."*

The last response of 'sure' shows non-neediness. Instead of trying to arrange and set in stone a date and a time, he chose instead to display non-neediness. This is something that a beautiful woman would do to you. The truth is that if she wants to see you, she will keep the night free and you will be able to arrange it later. Note that the above interaction is calibrated to the attraction stage and where you are unsure about her investment. If you already know that she likes you, then this is not the way to behave – you can show a little more interest. How did Mr. M know that he still needed to build attraction in the interaction above? Simply by the fact that she would not come to see him that night. (note that the full field report (with pictures) on how Mr. M picked up the Playmate is available HERE).

Frame Setting

A frame is an underlying assumption behind an interaction. For example, the frame of "Can I buy you a drink?" sets the underlying assumption that you are hitting on her. Compare this to the underlying assumption set by the words, "Hey, quick question, my friends and I were having a conversation... is it wrong to break up with someone via text message?" which sets the frame that you are just a guy asking a question.

There are various frames that you can set via text message which generate attraction. It is important that you understand that these are frames you should jump in and out of. Mix them up and do not stay on one frame to long. In general, the most useful frames to set are:

- That you and she do not get along (this causes sexual tension).
- That you are both attracted, but would be bad news for each other.
- That she is the sexual aggressor/sexual predator.
- That you are the prize (Done playfully or subtly).
- That she is trying to get you to like her or trying to win you over (whether it be in the sense of attraction, acceptance, or validation).
- That both of you are going to sleep together, but only if she lives up to your standards and expectations.

(Credit: Braddock, Mr M and The Attraction Forums)

Here are some examples of things that you can say over the phone or text (or indeed, in person) to set some of the frames above:

- "You're a player aren't you" (frame set: she is the sexual predator)
- "I need trust comfort and connection before we go there ;)" (frame set: she is trying to make you sleep with her. This is obviously a joke, but she will still qualify and accuse you of the same thing).
- "You're about to go into the lets just be friends zone" (frame set: you are the prize)
- "I'm not just a sausage with feet" (frame set: she is the sexual predator)

She may laugh at these frames, but laughing is an indication of passive acceptance of the frame. Any time that you can say something that achieves one of the above frames, you are likely to generate value and attraction.

(Mr M and Braddock will cover using frames in-field in depth in their upcoming Attraction ebook).

Getting Her to Take Positive Action

Building value and generating attraction through getting her to take positive action via text is a powerful strategy.

If you can get her to look something up on YouTube or Google, send you a picture, download a song, look at your facebook, add you on facebook or to simply do something for you while you are not there, then you are not there, then you are effectively causing investment. This is especially powerful over text and phone because it shows that even when you are not around, you can have a significant effect on her.

As a basic example, see how Mr M gains compliance over text, below:

> **Mr M:** *"Do you like the band 'Kings of Leon'?" [Note: you can use the name of any band you like]*
>
> **Her:** *"I don't know. I've never really heard of them."*
>
> **Mr M:** *"YouTube the song 'Notion'. My friend just wrote a song like it. Tell me if you like it?"*
>
> **Her:** *"Love it…"*
>
> **Mr M:** *"Awesome, right? What kind of music do you usually listen to?"*

The act of her checking the song Notion is almost as good as her spending time with you. This is because you are having an effect on what she is doing and giving her good emotions (by way of the song) even when you are not there. Never do more than one of these per week or so.

Other texts that you can send include:

> *"If you get in trouble… youtube 'how not to fake a heart attack' and do what this guy did… hilarious"*
>
> *"Omg. My ex decided to put live footage of how we met on youtube. Youtube 'can I get your number'."*
>
> *"Youtube or google 'Prank call Chinese Takeaway'. Voted funniest clip of 09"*
>
> *"The character of Mike Greenman from the video clip with his name (YouTube it!) is loosely based around my life lol"* [Note that this text message works best on a Short Fuse]
>
> *"OMG my brother is on a viral youtube video! Google 'evil eye baby'!!!"*
>
> *"Download Citizen Cope – Sideways….awesome song."*

"Go look at the video of me and my friends Vegas trip on facebook."

More Text Message Attraction Strategies

As investment increases, you can begin to push the envelope with your attraction material and really build your value. This must be calibrated, but can lead to great results, with much of your in-person attraction work being done for you with text or over the phone.

The following attraction tools in particular can be used to create a very high level of attraction over text message:

- Humor
- Role plays
- Push/pull
- Random childish jokes
- Callback humor
- Sexual baiting
- Sexual misinterpretation
- Light teasing
- Funny pet names
- Teasing names (dork, brat, etc)

Examples of Attraction Generating Text Message Exchanges

Example 1 - Amy: Using Callback Humor to Begin a Conversation

> Amy is from San Diego. When Braddock met her, he made jokes about the movie Anchorman (which is in San Diego). The opening text is a random funny line from a movie:
>
> **Braddock:** *"Hey did you know San Diego means, 'whale's Vagina'?"*
>
> **Amy:** *"Lol…. Jazz Flute is for little sissy fairy boys."*

Example 2 - Lisa: Using Disqualifying Humor

Dubbsy met Lisa and asked her some general questions, teased her, and qualified her. They found out they had some intersts in com mon; travel, reading, piano, and art. The bar was closing and Dubbsy told her that was the end of their first date and that we'd be goin on another one soon. Her friends dragged her away soon after because the bar was closing.

Dubbsy: *"You know what they call it when two people have the same interests and hobbies?"*

Lisa: *"What?"*

Dubbsy: *"They call it "you being a copycat." :-P "*

Lisa: *"LoL…shut it. If anything you copied me!"*

Dubbsy: *"No, I was born first so you copied me, sorry hunnie that's the rules. ;)"*

Lisa: *"Whatever, you're just jealous."*

Dubbsy: *"That is not how you spell "handsome." Lisa, with all that reading I'd expect you to at least know how to spell."*

Lisa: *"omg…hahaha whatever, at least I don't take people on dates to XXbar, sooo tacky!"*

Dubbsy: *"Well I've been thinking, we're going to have a theme to our second date, the theme will be "Make-ABaby," kinda like Build-A-Bear except not in a mall, unless that turns you on. ;)"*

Lisa: *"You are out of your mind!! Whatever happened to dinner and drinks and a movie?"*

Dubbsy: *"Lame. Yeah and maybe after we could go read books to the elderly. :-P"*

Lisa: *"lol shut up, what do you want to do?"*

Dubbsy: *"How good are you at pool and mini-basketball?"*

Lisa: *"I'll kick you ass, that's how good."*

Dubbsy: *"Careful you don't break your foot (buns of steel) ;-P You know where XX is?"*

Lisa: *"Yeah."*

Dubbsy: *"Ok Tuesday at 9. Bring your game face!!"*

Lisa: *"LoL!! >:-O…that's my game face..but I can't do Tuesday, how about Thursday at 9."*

Dubbsy: *"Yeah that works, don't think I don't know what you are doing…"*

Lisa: *"What am I doing?"*

Dubbsy: *"Pushing back the date so you can get your skills up!"*

Lisa: *"Hahahaha, noooo way! I'll beat you with both hands tied behind my back!"*

Dubbsy: *"Oooo I like where this is going ;)"*

Lisa: *"Shut up!! I didn't mean it like that, get your mind out of the gutter!"*

Dubbsy: *"LoL, you said it! I gotta run tho and get back to work."*

Lisa: *"ok have fun!!"*

Dubbsy: *"Don't tell me what to do! :-P"*

Lisa: *"hahahaha, fine don't then!"*

Dubbsy: *"Correct me if I'm wrong but that is still telling me what to do?"*

Lisa: *"LoL!!! Stop being such a smart ass!!*

Dubbsy: *"haha, ok ok ok you win this round (syke) ;-P ttys qt"*

Lisa: *"lol! Byyeee smartass!!*

Example 3 - Katie: Using Callback Humor and Banter to Create Attraction

Katie is a banker in her mid 20's. She and Braddock met at a club the week before. From the meeting, he found out that she's originally from Wisconsin. She has a nasally Northern accent and he teased her about
(a) being a greedy banker and
(b) having accounting thumbs. They also role played pretending to break up because of trust issues due to her being an evil banker. She teased him for being a farmer because he grew up in Oklahoma.

First Night, 1 Hour After Meeting:

Braddock: *"Nice meeting you Katie the banker. Don't stay out to late, you have a long day tomorrow. Foreclosing on an orphanage of blind kids, you'll need to be fresh!! :) -Braddock*

Katie: *"ha! You are ridiculous. Nice meeting you too Braddock."*

2 Days Later:

Braddock: *"Hi J.P. Morgan. I wish my boss would schedule this boring meeting right before I go to bed every night. (Yawn...)"*

Katie: *"LoL. I know what you mean! We have the worsssst meetings ever."*

Braddock: *"I stare and periodically nod, but all I hear is the mom on Charlie Brown talking... (whant whant... whant whant)."*

Katie: *"lol! You are funny farm boy."*

3 Hours Later

Katie: *"How did the meeting go? Did they move you to feeding chickens? ;)"*

Braddock: *"I wish! Turns out Pa needs me to brush the hog then help Ma churn butter for the big county fair coming up."*

Katie: *"LOL!!!"*

Braddock: *"Are you stealing pennies from the elderly or telling Tiny Tim's dad that he has to work an extra shift on Christmas eve. You know this could be Tim's last Christmas……."*

Katie: *"Who is tiny Tim?"*

Braddock: *"Wow…. missed the scrooge reference?!? Minus 3 cool points…good thing you are hot I guess…"*

Katie: *"Ohhhhh… wait!!! Now I remember the Christmas movie. Not fair, Tiny Tim threw me off."*

Braddock: *"They let retards play with people's money!?!? Hmmm… What bank do you work at again? Ok, back to work. Talk to you later brat. :)"*

Katie: *"LoLoL…Jerk!"*

The Next Day

Braddock: *"I'm sorry old woman, I don't care if you have nowhere else to go. I'm taking your house, so get out! (Said in a nasally Wisconsin accent to poor 90 year old woman)."*

Katie: *"I hate you! I don't have a nasally accent! (Ya'll farming today)."*

Braddock: *"My accent is sexy! Yours is too… If you think the mom off of Bobby's World sounds sexy. :)"*

Katie: *"LoL… Jerk! You watch too many cartoons! What are you doing this weekend?"*

Example 4 - Julie: Using Random Childish Jokes

Braddock has been texting Julie off and on for a few weeks. They met in Vegas, where she was a Long Fuse. Over time, he initiated text exchanges similar to the one below in order to generate attraction and get her to go from a Long Fuse to a Short Fuse.

Braddock: *"JuJuJuJulie! are you there?"*

Julie: "Hey! Yeah, I'm here...Soo bored. Flirt with me Oklahoma boy :)"

Braddock: "A). Don't tell me what to do...B). This is important."

Julie: "LoL...Ok, what's up?"

Braddock: "I just finished working out."

Julie: "LoL... ok."

Braddock: "I'm ridiculously sore."

Julie: "Poor baby! Do you want some cheese with that wine? Haha!"

Braddock: "I'm going to need you to organize a small army of your cutest girl buddies to cook me dinner and give me a massage. Ouch... Hurry! It's getting worse... P.S. Don't steal my jokes!!!!"

Julie: "Haha...A). No way! B). You are the one that steals my jokes! C). Why would I do that for you?"

Braddock: "Because I'm 23% more awesome today. Afterwards we can have a bible study. You can be the keynote speaker if you like..."

Julie: "Whatever! You don't deserve it! I do. Come give me massage... P.S..You, bible study?!? LOL Satan doesn't have bible studies."

Braddock: "Fine. I'll find another keynote speaker.. We'll trade, but I go first and keep your hands above the waist. I expect this to be all business. :)"

Julie: "lol...pg 13 for sure."

Example 5 - Alexis: The Power of Role Plays

Alexis is a med student Braddock met about a month ago, but had been unable to meet up with again as he was traveling so much. She is a Short Fuse based on the fact that he pushed things so far physiacally the night they met and by the way she is responding below:

Alexis: "Did you find a new love bunny in LA or what!? Did we really break up?

Braddock: *"We will NEVER break up. You took my virginity, as they say in the movie Highlander, "There can be only one!!!"*

Alexis: *"HAHA… you gotta be the only person who would reference Highlander in a text message. Ur a weirdo : p"*

Braddock: *"Ha. Don't fuck with me on movie trivia… I'm a man amongst boys."*

Alexis: *"I'll keep that in mind. Where u been hiding jerk face!? Thought a lion ate ur arm!"*

Braddock: *"I know I know… I've been on lock down the last few weeks."*

Alexis: *"And who has u on lock?"*

2 Hours Later

Braddock: *"Just been crazy busy with work… What are you up to?"*

Alexis: *"Pray for me, I have a Chem test 2day. Need a 96 for an A in the class!!!*

A Few Hours Later

Braddock: *"How did your test go?"*

Alexis: *"About to go take it! After my work out…"*

Braddock: *"Good luck. Kick some ass. Trample the weak and hurdle the dead!"*

Alexis: *"LOL… You are crazy! I'm putting that as my MySpace quote!"*

Braddock: *"Do you want me to text you the answers for your test?"*

Alexis: *"They convinscate phones… It's in the testing center… And I'm a genius anyways…Thanks though babe."*

Braddock: *"hmmm… "convinscate." LoL…. Your genius must be limited to Chem."*

Two Basic Rules for Building Value and Gaining Tempo over Text

1) Avoid Sending More Than One Text in a Row

As a general rule, do not send two texts in a row. If you have to do this, then you should call the second time. It shows decisiveness. If she does not pick up, allow her to reengage or simply contact her again in a couple of days with a funny text message or call.

2) End the Conversation First At Least 80% of the Time

You should always try to be the one to end the conversation. This keeps you from looking like a needy guy while texting. Ending a conversation is easy. You simply say, after a text exchange, 'Anyway, I've got friends over [or some other distraction that gives you value], so I better go. Spk soon [nickname]' or simply don't reply to her last text.

Alexis: "LoL… you jerk! I really am smart."

Braddock: "I know, you're one of the nerdiest girls I know… That's why I like you. Do you wear a pocket protector?"

Alexis: "Heck yeah I do!!! Every day in my scrubs… You are so mean!!!!!!"

Braddock: "Mooohaha."

Alexis: "Do u wear a fanny pack?"

Braddock: "Does Howdy Doody have wooden balls?!? Hell yeah I do. It's custom made. It's Italian leather with Braddock in rhinestones. It's a dual pocket 2 zipper comfort fit."

Alexis: "You are so weird! My dad use to say, "Does Raggedy Anne have cotton boobs!"

Braddock: "The answer to your dads question is "no". That's actually an urban legend. I believe her breasts are actually buttons."

Later That Night
Alexis: "When are u going to actually come hang out instead of working out ur thumbs all day?"

Braddock: *[In person we role played that we are still in junior high living with our parents]* "Dude, we gotta ask my mom… she's gonna say, "Go ask your dad." And he's gonna make us leave the door open and the lights on the whole time you are here…"

Alexis: "Well, tell them ur going to one of your buddy's houses and then just come stay with me. My parents are out of town this weekend."

Braddock: "Nice thinking."

Later On That Night

Alexis: "I'm going to bed. Good night, have a great day tomorrow."

[She then messaged me on MySpace]

Braddock: "Sending me messages on myspace? I thought you went to bed. How can we be together if you are gonna lie to me all the time?"

Next Morning

Alexis: "lol…you myspace stalking me last night? Hang out tonight, for real?"

Braddock: "Light stalking…lol. Tonight for sure. Can't til after 8. Cool?"

Qualification over Text Message

Deep qualification is usually best done either in person or over the phone. This is because it is similar to a 'getting to know her' phase which usually requires both parties to communicate in a fluid and unbroken fashion which text messages do not allow.

Qualifying over the phone is similar to qualifying in person. You can read Magic Bullets to get an idea of how this works or read Mr M's free article on Qualification on our website.

> Many mistake attraction and qualification as two separate phases. While they are different, attraction and qualification overlap and you can actually amplify attraction using qualification.

Qualifying over text message is trickier, but can and still should be done. There are two main ways in which you can use qualification in text messages. Note that qualification (including the 2 qualification techniques below) typically happens after you have value. This is due to the fact that the questions are more boring in nature and because she will not qualify unless she is somewhat invested. Qualification can be used very effectively to amplify the value that you already have.

1. The first way is to establish male to female attraction (i.e. telling her that you approve of something that she does). For example:

Sharon: *"[says something funny]"*

Mr M: *"Lol respect. You're actually funny. I like that. I think I'll let you be my sugar mama..."*

The key here is to qualify and give her validation or an indication of your approval or interest, but only after she has earned it. Do not over play this or she will do the opposite. Just subtly show signs of approval.

2. The second way is to mix in real qualifying questions in between fun banter or anytime after you know she is invested. This second strategy does not work well on Most Medium Fuses and almost not at all on Long Fuses. It is key that you have investment before firing these off. Below are simply examples of a few subtle qualifiers. For a longer list of qualification questions reference Magic Bullets:

Braddock: *"Tell me more about you.. 3 favorite things about Christmas?"*

Or...

Braddock: *"What kind of music do you like Texas girl? (Besides George Strait of course) :)"*

Or...

Braddock: *"Are you close to your family?"*

Or...

> ***Braddock:*** *[after she mentions a passion]*
> *"Why are you so passionate about X?"*

The trick with qualification is to thread them into normal conversation. You do not want to do 5 qualifiers in a row and let the conversation turn into an interview. Go back through the scripts in this book and see if you can notice where the dating coach subtly qualified the woman.

Remember that you must have a high level of investment before she will properly qualify herself. Also, remember that the best time to qualify is just after a high note, even if it seems like it's coming out of left field. Do not try to qualify on low notes in the text chain or out of nowhere after a large gap of time between your last communication.

Key Points of this Chapter

- There are eight main attraction triggers – Health, Social Intuition, Humor, Status, Wealth, Confidence, Pre-selection and Challenge.

- A key principle in Text and Phone Game is that the attraction triggers must be conveyed in such a way that they are either (a) secondary to, or a byproduct of, the subject matter of the text, (b) disguised by humor or (c) subtly woven into the subject matter.

- You have 'Tempo' in a text conversation if you are dictating the pace and tone of the communication and she is invested in your text messages.

- Two useful and basic rules for building value and gaining Tempo over text are: (1) Avoid sending more than one text in a row. (2) End the conversation first approximately 80% of the time.

- A frame is an underlying assumption behind an interaction. You can set frames via text message to generate attraction. Useful frames include: (1) That you and she do not get along, (2) That she is the sexual aggressor, (3) That you are the prize, (4) That she is trying to win you over and (5) That you will only sleep with her if she lives up to your standards.

- You can build value and generate attraction by getting her to take positive action and do something for you.

- You can use roleplays to bait her into sexual dialogue.

- Use qualification in Text and Phone Game by (a) giving her validation or an indication of your approval or interest but only after she has earned it and (b) thread normal qualification questions at high notes.

CHAPTER 8 - SEXUALIZATION

IN THIS CHAPTER:

- The Pro's and Con's of Sexualization

- Proper Sexualization

- The Key Concepts of Sexualization

- Power Ratio and Fuse Length

- Baiting and Mirroring Her Sexual Intent

- Sexual Hoops for Text and Phone Game

- False Barriers
  - Imaginary False Barriers
  - Real False Barriers

- Booty Call Phone and Texting

- Sexualization on the Phone

Chapter 8 - Sexualization

Introduction

'Sexualization' is the art of turning things sexual with a woman. Most people new to Love Systems are surprised at how quickly

(a) you can take things sexual in an interaction with a woman and
(b) the conversation can evolve from conservative and formal to explicit.

The phone is one of the best tools in your arsenal for tapping into a woman's sexual side. This is because it represents a safe medium for a woman to express her sexuality. Because there is no direct sexual dialogue in person, the phone represents a private way to show sexual desire without feeling judged or vulnerable. As your skill set increases, you will find that it gets easier and easier to introduce Sexualization into your Text and Phone Game.

There are large potential benefits in learning to properly sexualize your Text and Phone Game. Keep in mind however, that you can also destroy an encounter by sexualizing a conversation improperly.

While many of the examples and strategies outlined in this chapter may seem fun, interesting and exciting, remember that many times you will convert phone numbers to dates and all the way to sex without ever having to take things sexual through text or on the phone. Just because you want to take things sexual does not mean that you have to or that you should. Sexualization is only powerful under certain conditions. Outside of those conditions, trying to take things sexual can actually be quite toxic.

> Sexualization is playing with fire. While it is a powerful tool that can be used to take an interaction into a very sexual state, it is also very easy to ruin a phone number that would have very easily translated into a date by attempting to take things sexual too early.
>
> You can also do damage in your social circle if you are sexualizing conversations improperly.

As with all aspects of Love Systems (including Text and Phone Game) you want to put out the least amount of effort possible to progress to the next step. You do not get awarded bonus points for style or vulgarity.

Thus, try to see Sexualization as yet another club in your golf bag, to be used when the conditions call for it, but not as a random opportunity to talk dirty.

One thing you do need to internalize with Sexualization is that any and all girls can and will go sexual. We used to assume that only slutty girls would talk sexual, but after years of being a dating coach we quickly realized that all women will talk sexual under the right conditions. So, get it out of your head that, "X girl would never do that, she's different." You are wrong. She might not do it with you, but there is a guy out there who could get her to text things that would make you blush.

The Pro's and Con's of Sexualization

When trying to determine whether or not to take things sexual there are several factors to consider. Sexualizing a conversation is usually a 'high risk, high reward' strategy. This means that if it works, it can act as a catalyst to sex, making it easier for you to move the encounter quickly towards a sexual relationship. Once you get a woman to verbally commit through text or on the phone that she wants to have a sexual relationship with you, even if only under the veil of a role play, your work is greatly reduced when you next meet her in person. Dates will be less awkward and formal, and sometimes they can be skipped all together.

That being said, there are certain potential pitfalls of Sexualization. The incorrect use of Sexualization will immediately create a long fuse and typically leads to men being put into one of the following categories:

'Player'

Women may see you as a 'player' if you are good at Sexualization, but over use it. They will assume that your prime directive is to have sex with them, that you have sex with a lot of women and that you say the same lines to all women. While this can be helpful with a specific archetype of woman who is highly sexual and adventurous, it will hinder your chances with the majority of high quality women.

'Creep'

Many guys who are not good at the actual process of attracting and building comfort with women are adept enough at collecting phone numbers. If you skip the important steps of the Emotional Progression Model outlined in Magic Bullets (i.e. building attraction, qualifying and comfort in the initial interaction) and elect to go straight for Sexualization, assuming you had attraction when you really did not. The byproduct is usually that the woman will be uncomfortable with any kind of sexual dialogue. The result is obvious. She becomes uncomfortable, sees the guy as creepy, and might even become scared of him.

'Horny 7th Grader'

This is the guy who did everything right leading up to Sexualization and then messed up. He approached confidently, got the woman attracted to him, qualified her, and built comfort and connection. Now that she is comfortable with him, he decides to take things sexual over the phone. He baits her into something sexual and she is receptive to it. The dialogue goes well for a while. The problem is that he does not know when to cut off and switch topics. The result is that every conversation is extremely sexual. He cannot have a normal conversation and he cannot enjoy light sexual humor or even non-sexual humor. He comes across as the little boy who just discovered sex and has no depth of social interaction. Typically, he just keeps trying to take the dialogue dirtier and dirtier, regardless of the fact that she is obviously getting either annoyed or uncomfortable. The woman might even try to steer the conversation back into normal topics, however, he constantly steers things sexual every chance he gets.

Besides the obvious fact that this kind of behavior can be a major vibe killer, the more damaging effect is that is changes her perception of you. She may assume that her initial assumption about you was wrong and that you are actually just a juvenile guy who has not had sex in a long time and is easily excited by the prospect of merely talking about it. The key to avoiding being this guy is to have variation in your conversations. Do not go for Sexualization every time and develop your ability to use both sexual and non-sexual Callback Humor. Basically, develop the feel for when to cut it off.

Proper Sexualization

Know Your Desired Outcome

The first step in determining how sexual you should take things is to know your desired outcome with each woman. As there is a high level of risk involved in Sexualization, it is important that you determine the outcome that you desire and how much you are willing to risk with each woman you are talking to. You should ask yourself questions such as:

- Am I willing to potentially lose this woman in one 'all in' move?
- Do I just want to sleep with her or would I be upset if she cut off communication if things went bad?
- Is she in my social circle and would going sexual be a smart idea?
- Did we talk or joke about sexual topics when we first met so that taking things sexual over phone or text would be less of a big deal?
- Is the window to go sexual there, but I am avoiding it because I am playing it safe?

The answer to these types of questions is crucial for proper Sexualization.

The key is not to 'play it safe', but rather to 'play it smart'. If you are talking to a woman that you really like and hope to make your girlfriend, you should proceed with caution until you know for sure that
(a) she either sees you in the same light or
(b) you have enough relative value to be able to risk Sexualization and
(c) she responded well to the sexual baiting. If, on the other hand, you are dealing with a woman that you are just practicing with or are only interested in for sex, then a more risky approach would be appropriate. This is why it is crucial that you have a desired outcome in mind.

It is also recommended that you do not attempt to over sexualize text or phone conversations in your social circle if you are new to Love Systems or do not feel that you can competently use this technology yet. Regardless of how good you are with text and phone, it is always a good idea to work at a more controlled, 'chess instead of checkers' type approach in your social circle. This is not meant to imply that Sexualization is not a powerful tool that can be used on women in your social circle it is. However, it is twice as dangerous due to the collateral damage that it can cause to your wider social circle.

The Key Concepts of Sexualization

50:50 Power Ratio or Better

Determining what the 'Power Ratio' is between you and the woman is a great diagnostic tool that you can use in helping you to decide whether to go sexual or not. What is the Power Ratio? The Power Ratio is determined by fuse length, who has the most attraction, Tempo and emotional pull. If you are chasing her and she is hardly replying to your texts, then the Power Ratio is grossly in her favor. If she texts and calls you several times a day regardless of whether you reply or not, then obviously the Power Ratio is greatly in your favor. It basically comes down to who has the most interest in the other. For example, a 50:50 power ration represents mutual levels of interest.

It is a good rule of thumb to only take things sexual when the Power Ratio is in your favor. At a minimum, you should be on equal ground. In the preceding chapters we discussed categorizing each phone number as either a Short, Medium, or Long Fuse. You can assume that a 60:40 or better Power Ratio in your favor is a Short Fuse, a 40:60 or worse Power Ratio in her favor is a Long Fuse and anything in between is a Medium Fuse.

> ### The Changing and Unpredictable Nature of Power Ratios
>
> Note that before you have sex, Power Ratios are constantly changing. One day she may think that you are amazing and she cannot wait to see you. The next day, her ex-boyfriend could pop back up in her life, which significantly decreases your Power Ratio. The key is to realize that circumstances occur which change the Power Ratio without warning. All of a sudden, your sexual banter that she once loved is no longer well received. This does not mean that you are out of the game. It does, however, mean that you need to respect the shift in Power Ratio and tone down any sexual banter for now.
>
> Remember - women live in the emotional moment. This means that they may be willing to talk dirty today, but they may be disgusted by it tomorrow. You may even have sex with a girl one night that is not willing to talk sexual the next day. Accept this as part of the variable nature of the game.

Why would we say "do not take things sexual when the Power Ratio is not in your favor"? Have you ever had a woman that you were not attracted to try to kiss you or try to talk sexual to you? If so, then you probably already know the uncomfortable feeling that this creates. You may have never really thought about how you were not attracted to her, but when she made it clear she was in fact attracted to you, it forced your logical mind to confirm in fact that you were not, which put the final nail in the coffin of her chances with you.

Similarly, if there is one thing that will quickly kill a phone number that might have been salvageable down the road, it is taking things sexual too fast or at the wrong time. If she is not attracted to you yet, does not see you as a potential sexual partner, is not in the mood to talk sexual, or there is simply not enough comfort between the two of you, then going sexual will do nothing but push you further away from your goal. This is why respecting the Power Ratio is so important.

Also, remember that a woman can go from a Short Fuse, to a Long Fuse, back to a Short Fuse multiple times. If she was a Short Fuse who was receptive to Sexualization, but for whatever reason is showing Long Fuse tendencies, do not sexualize at that time.

Power Ratio and Fuse Length

<u>Short Fuse</u>

The shorter the fuse, the higher the Power Ratio and the more likely it is that she will be willing to go sexual with you. When you have a Short Fuse and a good Power Ratio, you will notice that you can usually move through the Sexual Hoops (described later on in this chapter) quickly. She will give you a larger margin of error due to the high level of investment that you have from her. This means that if you go to sexual or go sexual to early, she will give you more warning signs and not immediately become a Medium Fuse or Long Fuse. However, if you 'over sexualize' and do not read the signs she is not comfortable with it, you can quickly turn a Short Fuse to Long Fuse or even lose her entirely.

<u>Medium Fuse</u>

If you have between a 50:50 and 60:40 Power Ratio, you are usually safe to at least introduce a sexual theme using the sexual baiting techniques described below to see where she stands. However, proceed with caution. Start by playfully baiting her to see if she is willing to go sexual or not.

In a Medium Fuse situation, you must be disciplined enough not to over sexualize until she is ready. A Medium Fuse can quickly become a Long Fuse if you are not careful and push the Sexualization too far. By the same token, good Sexualization can take a Medium Fuse to a Short Fuse quickly.

Long Fuse

If you are currently at a 40:60 or worse Power Ratio, then any kind of sexual vibe will likely do more harm than good. In this situation, avoid Sexualization until your Power Ratio and fuse length changes. Any time that you feel that you have less than a 50/50 Power Ratio, trying to turn things sexual will make her feel like you are emotionally leaking, or that you lack social intuition and do not understand that you are being weird. With Sexualization (and with game in general) you must not leak emotionally. It is ok for her to know that you want her, but you will lose a massive amount of attraction if she ever thinks that you need her. A key concept that is covered in the revolutionary INNER GAME SENINAR is that want is ok but need causes death in attraction.

As previously stated, you may have to burn a Long Fuse down to a Medium Fuse over weeks or even months. No matter how long it takes, you must wait until she is at least a Medium Fuse and you have an advantageous Power Ratio before introducing Sexualization.

Baiting and Mirroring Her Sexual Intent

In the early stages of Sexualization, it is crucial that you move only as fast and as far as she is comfortable with. A good way to view it is to think of her Sexualization comfort level as a staircase. Early on, you must climb the staircase one stair at a time. At the top of each stair you will need to gauge her comfort level (or lack thereof) before moving to the next step. If you sense that she is not comfortable going further, then it simply means that you should burn the fuse down more or save Sexualization for the phone or in person. That being said, depending on her responses, you may find yourself skipping multiple stairs after just a few texts.

> **TIP:** Do not be over zealous with Sexualization. Instead, adapt your game plan to the type of woman that you are talking to.
> Bait to see where she stands.

So how do you know if you should move back a step, stay on one step, move forward slowly, or sprint up the staircase? You test comfort levels by 'sexually baiting' to see if and how she responds. Baiting her simply means throwing out extremely subtle, flirtatious jokes, comments, innuendos, misinterpretations, role plays or references of a sexual nature and seeing whether she 'bites' or not. If she takes the bait, by either playing along or by furthering the sexual dialogue with a sexual comment of her own, then this is a sign telling you that it is ok to move up the staircase. You will know it is time to move up because you will notice that she is comfortable with you opening a dialogue which was not previously available.

If you are baiting properly then it should be no cause for concern if she rejects the bait. In your early texts, the bait should be so subtle that if she chooses not to take it, you should be left no better and no worse off than before the bait was dangled. However, if you get an overly negative reaction, this probably means that you crossed the line by attempting to climb too many stairs at once.

A Note on Baiting

Baiting is not simply making an overly sexual shot in the dark and hoping 'just maybe' she will go for it and talk dirty. The worst case scenario is that baiting for Sexualization should leave you right where you started. Baiting is merely hinting at something more sexual to see if she is willing to go there with you. In fact, early baiting is so subtle she should almost not notice the temperature change.

A good rule of thumb is to bait and then mirror her sexual intent or playfulness for at least a few texts. Do not verbalize too much more sexual intent or playfulness than she is willing to give you. If you bait her sexually and find that she is not willing to go sexual at all, then you should back off temporarily by ignoring it and/or changing the subject. Backing off does not mean apologizing for it. If she is only comfortable with intermittent sexual joking then you should only sexually joke with her on that frequency. Be patient with Sexualization and take what she gives you. If you feel she is ready to speed things up, then go for in and take some chances. If you get the vibe that she is not biting on the Sexualization, then simply slow down. If she starts making statements of direct sexual interest or intent after baiting, then and only then, should you consider making statements of direct sexual interest and intent. The tactic is to simply bait her sexually, wait for her response and mirror her willingness to take things sexual and gradually start pushing the envelope slightly farther. Remember, this does not mean that you are waiting for her to lead things sexually. She will be unlikely do this. You must always be leading. However, you want to lead gradually, not boldly. You lead gradually through baiting and then mirroring her to determine your next response and by knowing when you should be pulling back before things make her uncomfortable and by cycling things back to normal conversation.

Sexual Hoops for Text and Phone Game
(Credit Dahunter for Original Sexual Hoops Concept)

Sexual Hoops are a powerful tool which can be used to turn conversations sexual. They were originally designed for use infield but can be adapted to Text and Phone Game. For information on how to use Sexual Hoops specifically in field, see Mr M and Braddock's upcoming Attraction ebook. This section will focus on the use of Sexual Hoops in Text and Phone Game. Sexual Hoops uses baiting and operates much like qualification hoops. The idea is to introduce small hoops at first and gradually work up to larger and larger hoops. Each sexual hoop that she agrees to, or plays along with, builds sexual compliance and opens the door for you to push the envelope.

Sexual Hoops: Stage 1

The first stage of Sexual Hooping consists of exaggerated and/or unrealistic Sexual Hoops. These are based on completely unrealistic statements or role plays which are usually humorous. Everything that you say is based on fiction, which leaves her with little doubt that you are actually joking and makes it fun for her to play along. The best vehicle to deliver these Sexual Hoops is through role plays, exaggeration, and playful unrealistic accusations. These can also be conveyed by making obvious misinterpretations of the things she texts to you or by making obvious misinterpretations of things that took place when you two talked in person. The lines below will make zero sense if they are just fired off at random. They must be threaded into a conversation and have at least some relevance. One easy way to do this is to state something sexual and then disqualify yourself in a funny, obviously non true way. While we will provide examples below, take the time to go back and look at the text game exchanges throughout this book and see if you can notice the Sexual Hoops real time.

Examples of roles you can take on for the first level of Sexual Hoops:

- *If I wasn't gay and celibate it would so be on.*

- *[When talking about hanging out] "My mom said if your mom will bring you over then my mom will take you home. But no making out in the back seat…This rule will be strictly enforced." Or, "We can hang out but, we have to leave the door open and the light on if we watch a movie. My mom doesn't trust girls like you."*

- *Thank God I'm a moral rock, because you are bad.*

- *Shy guy. "I really wanted to kiss you when we met, but I'm scared of girls."*

- *Marry and divorce her over being bad or good in bed.*

- *Marry and divorce, but keep getting back together for the amazing makeup sex.*

Examples of misinterpretations you about the first time you met in first level Sexual Hoops:

- *[When she obviously didn't try to make out with you] "I can't believe you tried to make out with me in front of all of my friends. You don know I'm from the Bible belt. I have to wait for marriage before second base."*

- *"You know, I'm glad we met, you're really cute, and funny…but next time can we actually have a conversation and you not stare at me like a piece of meat. I'm not just a sex object."*

- *"Just so we are clear, stop means stop. I don't want to have to call the cops like last time."*

- *"I liked talking to you tonight but I'm a little disappointed that you were trying to get in my pants all night… 'No means no' Sara."*

- *[Bolder, maybe for an extremely Short Fuse] "I liked talking to you tonight, you're really sexy, but I'm a little disappointed that you didn't try to get in my pants."*

- *"You drunk text me and tried to smooth talk me into coming to meet you [even if she did not do this, it is a funny accusation]. Lucky I'm a moral rock."*

- *"Listen, I'm obviously attracted to you too, but I need trust comfort and connection before you get in my pants. [Awesome if said to a girl that you were obviously trying to escalate.]*

TIP: Imagine Sexual Hoops Stage 1 as a cartoonist's illustration of you and her having sex, it's supposed to be funny and crazy, but not dangerous enough that she could react negatively. It is merely a joke that happens to involve sexual innuendo. When using these jokes, the more outrageous, the better.

Note that these lines are mostly used in the context of a conversation so that they do not seem staged or inappropriate.

Notice also the framing that occurs in these statements. You are often trying to frame her as the sexual aggressor. An example of a text interaction involving first level Sexual Hoops and framing would be:

Natalie: *"I had fun last night. ;)"*

Braddock: *"I had fun too, but I'm glad you didn't try to make out with me. I'm a moral rock you know. You are going to have to move slow with me..."*

Natalie: *"LoL...I totally agree. I'm sorry if I moved to fast."*

Braddock: *"It's cool. Just don't let it happen again ok? Kissing before the 23rd date makes baby Jesus cry ;)"*

Sexual Hoops: Stage 2

The 2nd stage consists of semi-realistic Sexual Hoops. These hoops are loosely reality based and are typically used after she begins to realize what your intentions are. Note that these are only introduced if she plays along with the 1st stage hoops and has also shown interest in meeting up. While it is becoming obvious you want to have sex with her, it is normally a good idea to follow these up with a disqualifier or to mix them with humor.

A disqualifier and/or humor may be important to soften the statements of your early Sexual Hoops. Once she takes the bait again and again and you can tell that you two are well beyond just non serious role plays, you can drop the humor and disqualifiers more often.

A Note on Drunk Dialing

A girl calling you late at night when she is drunk is often a great time to introduce sexual themes. Oftentimes, when a girl gets drunk, she can express herself sexually and not feel responsible for it because she was drunk. This does not mean that you should assume that just because a girl is drunk that she wants to talk sexual, but you can bait her using Sexual Hooping and see what she says.

Examples of the second level of sexual hoop are lines such as:

- *"We would be bad for each other. This would be all fights and makeup sex."*

- *"Love the dress in your facebook pic…I kinda want you to take my virginity."*

- *"Next time I see you will begin/end in a heavy makeout….Sorry, it's your fault."*

These lines happen in the context of the text conversation. An example of a text interaction involving second level Sexual Hoops would be:

Maria: *"So what exactly are we doing tonight?"*

Braddock: *"That's a surprise… P. s. wear those sexy Gucci heels you wore last time"*

Maria: *"Hmmm…ok. You love those on me huh?"*

Braddock: *"Those shoes and a short black skirt could lead to bad things…if I wasn't a moral rock… ;)."*

Notice how the intent to hook up is more obvious, but still buffered by disqualification and humor (i.e. while Braddock said that the shoes and skirt could lead to bad things, he still made a humorous disqualification and humor (i.e. while Braddock said that the shoes and skirt could lead to bad things, he still made a humorous disqualification by telling her that he was a moral rock).

Sexual Sexual Hoops: Stage 3

The 3rd stage of Sexual Hoops is sexually challenging hoops. Before using these, it is important to make sure that you have properly led the woman through stages 1 and 2. Only if she has been receptive to the first 2 stages should you continue to stage 3 of Sexual Hoops.

Depending on the situation, sexually challenging hoops can either be playful or serious. When using the playfully challenging hoops, you playfully mock her sexual abilities or frame her sexual abilities as not being able to keep up with you. You an also challenger her on things you will do to her. The idea is to get her to playfully joust with you in a way that gets her qualifying to you on how good she is sexually.

This is a very powerful tool if utilized properly. If she is not interested, she will likely deflect the playful hoop or just not acknowledge it. However, if she is sufficiently attracted and she enjoyed the first hoops, she will likely play along and willingly conspire to build the sexual tension by qualifying herself or by playfully qualifying you back. In Stage 3 Sexual Hoops you can qualify what you will/would do to her or challenge her to qualify herself sexually.

Here are a few examples of playfully challenging Sexual Hoops:

"You couldn't keep up with me."

"I should have kissed you last night."

"You're probably a bad kisser!"

"Come spoon me."

"Come make out with me."

"kinda couldn't stop thinking about kissing you last night…"

"1 to 10 scale…how good of a kisser are you?"

"1 to 10 scale…how good are you in bed?"

"Haha you're too much of a nice girl, I'd make you blush."

"Hot girls are always bad in bed."

"I'm going to do bad things to you next time I see you."

"I'm going to rip your clothes off when I see you."

"You're a good kisser…B+….maybe even A-…I was impressed."

"What are you wearing?"

It is important to remember that these should be said in a flirty, playful manner. If you come across as uptight and serious, you are either going to hurt her feelings or annoy her, or come across weird. Level 3 Sexual Hoops must be well timed. Level 3 Sexual Hoops must be woven into already sexualized conversation. Jamming them into random conversation will back fire. Make sure you get comfortable using the first and second level hoops and are consistently getting good responses before you start using level 3 and 4.

There is also a time and a place for more serious sexually challenging hoops. You should only use these hoops when the conversation has truly become sexual to a level where introducing a playful vibe would actually kill the sexual mood. This means that she has gradually, yet consistently verbalized sexual intent with you and she is blatantly not joking. This allows you to make more declarative sexual challenges and statements of intent. The goal is to create sexual tension that cannot be resolved until the next time you see each other. It is not a declaration of sexual hopes and dreams that you 'wish' you could fulfill. Rather, it is the creation and recognition of the obvious sexual tension that you both feel, and then challenging her on it.

<u>Example of Sexual Hoops Levels 1-3 by, Love Systems Instructor, Daxx:</u>

Sara is a bartender Daxx met through cold approach. They had a short, but sexually charged interaction before exchanging phone numbers. They met up at a different club after she got off work. They did not get to meet up that weekend, but continued to build attraction and sexualize through text. They would eventually meet up in Las Vegas.

In this example Daxx pushes through the Sexual Hoops hard and fast. He did this for a couple of reasons. Firstly, he was only going to be in town for a few nights and was not sure if he would be able to see her again. Secondly, Sara is extremely witty and she responded in a manner that gave him a green light to push things sexual right away. If she had given different responses, he would have pulled back on the reins.

Daxx does a great job of moving through the Sexual Hoops while building in role plays, humor, and moving things forward logistically. This is a great example of just how fast things can ramp up sexually. (Some of these texts seem long. This is because Daxx has a Black Berry that allows typing of unlimited characters and then sends them in 144 character messges. Some of these were sent as one message, but received as 2 or 3 back to back messages.).

Daxx: *"You are fucking trouble.."*

Sara: *"you don't even know me, and you've already figured me out..."*

Daxx: *"If we don't meet Sunday we're breaking up & I'm seeing other people... :)"*

Sara: *"You're rather bossy, English..."*

Daxx: *"We would never work out, it would be all fights & make up sex.."*

Sara: *"hmm, yes. but both arguably have merit. and the latter is usually quite fun...;)*

Daxx: *"As long as the other person's favourite position isn't the star fish.. What's yours, and don't say flying penguin cos that's mine?"*

Sara: *""favourite"? you are so British....and I have simple tastes when it comes to positions. shove me against a wall and I'm happy."*

Daxx: *"That would be hot.. its just a shame we aren't attracted to each other & have no chemistry.. ;)"*

Sara: *"If I'm going to do something hot, I'm going to do it 100% hot..."*
Daxx: *"You don't know what you're getting yourself into....I want to see you soon.....Make it happen."*

Sara: *"again with the bossy....I'll be at underground again after work, new earings...."*

(She gets off work and her and a friend meet Daxx and his friends at an after hours club. Daxx and her makout, but they do not go home together)

(Next Night)

Daxx: *"Heading to (random club) to meet some friends...Come play"*

Sara: *"English, as much as I would love to discuss the merits of the flying penguin with you in person, I have to be at work at 5:30am to analyze some media...will you break up with me now that you know I'll always put my career first? ;)"*

Daxx: *[It's his last night in town so he pushes hard] "Fine...I'm gonna go have a drink with my buddies & coming over to crash at your house after. You can hang out too...I guess. Hands above the waist ;)"*

Sara: *"LoL....ooooh really?! if my alarm wasn't set for 4:20am....maybe we are destined to only have a text and/ or facebook romance....sigh."*

Daxx: *"American girls = All talk. Probably better we don't see each other as it you'd need to be able to walk for work tomorrow.. ;)"*

Sara: *"rather cocky, aren't we luv? and while this American girl may appear to be all talk, she knows that if we did see each other, you would fall in love, move here, and try to co-own a dog with her....;)"*

Daxx: *"His name would be James (he would undoubtedly be a good boy) he & I would be best friends (but he probably wouldn't like you) and he would be a french bulldog. But anyway enough of you changing the subject.. :) Add me on facebook sexy – Kev Daxx. Look after the kids while I'm gone."*

(Daxx flys back to Los Angeles and they continue flirting through text. She happens to jump right back into the sexual hoops. If she had not, it would have been better advised to build things back up over time).

Sara: *"luv, ive been craving a flying penguin and the kids miss you... hop a cab and come back to the chi...I'll pay the fare ;) ps- bring James"*

Daxx: *"In the cab on my way.. James said he'll come.. but only cos I'm coming. If work wasn't your religion the flying penguin would be in full flow.."*

(At this point they are going back and forth between the first and third sexual hoops. While they are role playing, you can feel the sexual tension and sexual intent. They both mean what they are saying, but the jokes infused in the banter keep it from getting to serious).

Sara: *"I've reconsidered. good banter is too hard to come by. fuck the career, I'll take the FP...but only if you promise to talk dirty and keep up the biting. love an english accent and a good, hard bite..."*

Daxx: *"You are bad for me. Why didn't you see me in Chicago... First girl I've actually liked in the states.. What a waste."*

Sara: *"I didnt fall in love with you until Sunday at midnight..sigh. 1sr girl in the states!? sugar, I can run better game than that..but make you a deal; fly back and stay at my place. we can play above the waist and yahtzee..."*

Sara: *"or give that starfish a whirl..though, I would prefer feet on the ground and facing away. better angle for hair pulling and ass smacking. ugg...total waste is right."*

Daxx: *"Hair pulling & ass smacking.. not forgetting neck biting. Standing reverse starfish is our new signature move.. It's probably a good thing we don't live near each other because we would never get anything done…"*

Sara: *"we would get one thing done...and I told you sugar, if we would have met up, you'd never want to leave. that, and I'd never stop biting and sucking on your bottom lip to let you. (Cant lie, was a bit intrigued by it.)"*

Daxx: *"You need to come stay in LA sexy but I'm warning you there will be a lot of biting.."*

Sara: *"can your cell receive picture texts?"*

Daxx: *"I can on my other cell (sent #)."*

Sara: "two phones?! not sure I'm buying that....shame, I was going to send you something so you would have a good visual of what you would be biting"

Daxx: "I'm english, have you not heard of James Bond? What you don't think he'd have 2 phones.. Are you calling me a pussy? Good thing you're hot:)"

Sara: "oh yeah, thank god ive at least got that going for me...;) and still not buying the 2 cells, 007. let's try email? and lucky you're witty and have a sexy mouth..."

Daxx: "(sent email) Now send the pics or you'll never see James again:)"

Sara: "your weak, British threats don't scare me, luv. but one tease is forthcoming...ps-I admire your attempt to redirect to your "2nd phone"..;) ha!"

Daxx: "Silly American Girl who never travels. Cell #1 is my US number so it doesn't cost $1million to text, Cell #2 is my world phone... But on a serious note, before I forget...I need you to take care of James this weekend so me & my buddies can go to Vegas & comb the desert for hookers & cocaine. He's not old enough for that yet, maybe next year P.P.S. Can't wait to see these pics..."

Sara: "sugar, this American girl used to travel through europe, but she did it without a cell phone. and can you put James on a train to the chi, or do I need to come pick him up? hookers and coke = $$, but not for my little guy. don't want him to become jaded."

Daxx: "I'd do the traveling without a cell thing too if I had no friends to keep in contact with.. smartass ;) James can't ride the train alone yet. You can come pick him up, but you should know that your pics are making it difficult for me to not think about doing bad things to you when you get here.."

Sara: "sigh, I do enjoy "bad things"...hmm, when are they deporting you?I didn't mention it, because i didnt wantyou to rush out and buy a ring, but im hitting up vegas or LA with some buddies before Xmas, and last I heard, LA was the front runner. Also headed to a little place called Aspen in Jan, but I doubt you English boys know how to snowboard..."

Daxx: *"Don't make me come to Aspen & show your ass up on the snow blondie. We're gonna be in Vegas 4th-8th December, other than that in LA til 14th Dec then home to London for xmas. When you coming sexy? I better see you while you're here or I'll be mad.. :) Even though you've already started planning for my bday, I'd like an Audi R8 this year."*

Sara: *"junior, start streching now. that reverse, standing starfish is going to happen sooner than anticipated...."*

Daxx: *"Good thing I was born ready. Get here soon... Readyyyyy go"*
Sara: "English, you have no idea how much I need a good, hard bite right now. add some naughty talk in that sexy accent.....grrrr."

Daxx: *"You need to get your ass to LA so we can ruin each other.. I hope you know what you're getting yourself in to hottie."*

Sara: *"all I know is that what I'm getting into has a smart mouth, likes to bite, and has an upper body I would push my grandmother into traffic to get my hands on. travel plans are in the works"*

Sexual Hoops: Stage 4

The 4th stage of Sexual Hoops is graphic sexual intent.

At this point, you should have moved the past the first three hoops and received receptivity and compliance from her on each hoop. The conversation must have switched to sexual and the vibe must feel 'on'. You are still going to disqualify every once in a while but the disqualification will be softer. These hoops are basically dirty talk. Remember to go back and forth between all 4 levels of hoops. Just because you are on hoop four does not mean you can not jump back down to hoop one, two, or three.

It is very important that you remember Level 4 Sexual Hoops are not necessary to get a date or to sleep with the woman. In most cases, if your Sexualization has progressed this far, you should have already met up with the woman and taken things further in person. We highly suggest that you avoid these until you have mastered the other principles in this book. Using these incorrectly can absolutely kill a situation that was otherwise good.

Example of Sexual Hoops Levels 1- 4 (By Braddock)

This example is jumping the middle of a conversation that has been going going on for a while. Braddock met Amy while she was working as a stripper. She has a boyfriend but Braddock and her have hung out a few times and escalated physically, but not to the point of sex. This example is great because it shows just how far you can take things and just how much women will open up and share their most inner fantasies to a guy that is willing to go there.

Amy: "Hi hotness :) How was your xmas.?"

Braddock: "Christmas was awesome…You? Did you get coal in your stocking again?"

Amy: "LoL…no! My xmas was awesome. I got a really bad ass digital camera."

Braddock: "What did you get me for Christmas?!?! When is our next make out (I mean) movie session? Kinda miss your face…"

Amy: "Ahahah what did I get you? Hmmm..I say a crazy Vegas trip with lots of champagne, glitter, cigars, and gambling…which will then lead to more insane activities. :) You kinda miss my face? I kinda miss yours too."

Braddock: "If you and I went to Vegas I would be primarily focused on trying to get you pregnant. ;)"

Amy: "BRADDOCK!!!! AHAHAHAHAHAHA great…I know I just had my bday and my clock is ticking but I don't wanna have any demon babies just yet!"

Braddock: "lol…Your cute and I'm ridiculously good looking. We would make pretty demon babies."

Amy: "Ahahahaha that's very true :)"

Braddock: "How old are you now?"

Amy: "26."

Braddock: *"I'm older than you....so I'm still the boss of you and you have to do what I say..."*

Amy: *"Ahahaha...you're the boss of me? Hmmmm...I kinda like it."*

Braddock: *"I don't like your attitude...go to my room."*

Amy: *"lololol.. Did you guys get snowed in? I kept seeing cnn reports about snow there."*

Braddock: *"Soo much snow. Didn't leave my brothers house for 2 days."*

Amy: *"Niiice, that's awesome. I would have rolled in the snow with you. Hehe."*

Braddock: *"Snowball fights ending in snowball makeup sex?"*

Amy: *"Yah cause I'm sure you'd end up socking me square in the face with a snowball, and then I'd get mad, stalk inside, skulk, spill tea on you on purpose and so yeah....hahahah."*

Braddock: *"lol....let's do it. There has been a build up between us.... when/if/when we ever do have sex..it's going to be so fucking hot....just sayin..."*

Amy: *"Thanks Braddock, keep reminding me of this...and how I kept catching my bf watching porn this week. God damn it!"*

Braddock: *"Good...I wanted you to be sexually frustrated until next time I see you."*

Amy: *"You are bad...bad...bad..."*

Braddock: *"What's your hottest sexual experience?"*

Amy: *"Be more specific..."*

Braddock: *"One where you were like... "FUCK that was hot..."*

Amy: *"hmm...probably the time this guy I was dating cut my underwear off with a knife. Come to think of it, we didn't even fuck that night, we just messed around...."*

Braddock: "That's intense...Rape fantasy?"

Amy: "Not like rape...but similar to that whole power, voracious type feeling."

Braddock: "Choked and spanked?"

Amy: "lol...yes that stuff is definitely on my likey list."

Braddock: "Ok...now you are DEFINITELY in trouble and DEFINITELY go to my room..."

Amy: "Ahahahahaha and you're DEFINITELY getting me all excited! And I just got to stupid work!"

Amy: "You are Satan."

Braddock: "Hot and bothered? I bet you are sexy as hell when you dance now. You're welcome."

Amy: "Oh you suck! I'm so turned on right now...God you suck!"

Braddock: "Send me a pic of you in your outfit...you are a bad mother fucker in your dancer gear..."

Amy: "OMG you are hot...there is nobody here, come get me I want to fuck you so bad..."

Braddock: "Sorry...I'm 3 states away..."

Amy: "What!?!? You aren't in LA!? Grrrr... When do you come back!?!?!?"

Braddock: "Tomorrow."

Amy: "OMFG"

Braddock: "You've got me turned on now...what a waste."

Amy: "Um yeah...this is alllll your fault Braddock."

Braddock: "Totally blame you..."

Amy: *"You were asking me questions first!!!"*

Braddock: *"Well...don't give me hot answers that make me want to fuck your brains out."*

Amy: *"LoL...well it's not my fault that I like what you like.. Here's your pic. Don't you wish you were here now?"*
[sends a pic of her bent over the stage]

Braddock: *"Seriously making me hard right now....fuck."*

Amy: *"mmm...No Midwest booty to ring?"*

Braddock: *"Not with an ass and stalkings like that..."*

Amy: *"Ahahaha..That's right baby!"*

Amy: *"God damn it....3 states away...why aren't you here? I seriously want you inside me."*

Important Notes on Sexual Hoops

- Just because you have progressed from one stage to the next, does not mean that you should abandon the hoop or hoops below that stage. An ideal strategy would be to progressively unlock one hoop at a time while still continuing to jump back and forth between the previously unlocked hoops.

- When using Sexual Hoops, remember that a woman lives in the emotional moment. So just because you had a woman texting or talking on the phone at Stage 3 of Sexual Hoops on one night, it does not necessarily mean that you should jump right back into that same level of hoop the next day. A better strategy would be to back up a few hoops and slowly reintroduce the hoops to work back up to your previous level.

- Do not try to blast through hoops too fast. While it is possible to quickly progress to the fourth stage in just a few texts or on one call if the fuse is short enough, you will see that it is much more common that these stages happen over a few weeks, or even months depending on her fuse length. So, for example, it may be only after a date or two that she feels more comfortable being sexual and thus progressing through the hoops.

- Just like getting off the phone first, it is important that you are the one who ends the Sexualization first. If you go sexual and she has to stop you (or she stops responding), this is usually a sign that you are moving too fast. The ideal situation would be to get things extremely sexual and at a peak, then leave her hanging by telling her that you have to go or by changing the subject. This way, you also keep Tempo.

Sexual Hoops Summary

Sexual Hooping is a powerful technique. The idea is that you take the woman through the 1st hoop, which is a playful sexual introduction. If she accepts this, then you proceed to the 2nd hoop, which is grounding your sexual intentions to reality. If she accepts this, then you take her through the 3rd hoop and get her to qualify herself to you sexually. If that hoop is well received then you move on to the final hoop, where you start sharing graphic sexual intent.

The Sexual Hoop stages described above were designed to be use as a gradient ladder to help you escalate the interaction gradually towards a sexual context. With practice, you will start to recognize when you can skip stages. Until then, we highly recommend that you abide by each stage.

> TIP: Do not be too concerned with how fast you progress through Sexual Hoops. You do not get points for speed or style and you want to do most of your sexual escalation in person.

False Barriers

Having a barrier to hooking up is a powerful way to build sexual tension. Most famous love stories have barriers for the hero and heroine to overcome to become romantically involved (e.g. Romeo and Juliet, The Notebook, etc). The barriers are what make the romance exciting. We are using the same principle here. False Barriers are real or playful reasons why you both cannot act on your sexual intent or attraction. They are basically admitting that you want each other, but highlighting a real or playful reason for why the two of you can not act on it. There are also a few other important reasons why False Barriers are important to use:

- False Barriers can take the edge off strong sexual comments if they are used in conjunction with Sexual Hooping. A Sexual Hoop without a false barrier can often make the woman feel uncomfortable. When we use a false barrier, it takes some of the bite out of the sexual comment. False Barriers are not necessary every time we deliver a sexual hoop, but should be utilized any time your message could be misunderstood as uncomfortably sexual, or if you think your message by itself might convey that you are 'emotionally over reaching' (a concept covered in the revolutionary INNER GAME SEMINAR– also see Mr M's free post on Emotional Overreaching HERE).

- False Barriers are also used to stay out of the pursuer frame. This does not mean that showing interest puts you in the pursuer frame. There is a difference in showing that you are interested and attracted, versus being the pursuer who is chasing so hard that it feels more like begging than expressing your sexual intent like a man. An ideal situation or frame would be one where the woman is chasing you an equal amount or slightly more than you are chasing her. False Barriers allow us to better meet this end by setting the frame that she too has to work to make getting together happen.

How to use False Barriers

Imaginary False Barriers

False Barriers can be real or imaginary. 95% of the time, you will use imaginary false barriers. You can attach these to the beginning or the end of a sexual hoop. Examples include:

> ***Braddock:*** *"We could never date, it would be all fights and make up sex."*
>
> ***Braddock:*** *"If I wasn't a virgin, I totally would have tried to make out with you last night."*
>
> ***Braddock:*** *"You're fucking hot and I totally want to rip your clothes off, but I'm waiting for marriage."*

> **Braddock:** "I'm really attracted to you and I really like you, but I can't date you unless you are rich."
>
> **Braddock:** "I would totally try to have sex with you, but I recently swore a vow of celibacy. Sorry."
>
> **Braddock:** "Just so you know, we can only go to third base after my father receives a sizeable dowry and the pre nup has been signed."
>
> **Braddock:** "Look, I think you're cute but I'm pretty sure baby Jesus would be upset if we dated. I just want to avoid another locust plague."
>
> **Braddock:** "I would totally rip your clothes off, but I get really nervous around girls. I'll need a brown paper bag to breathe into."

In the examples above, observe how the False Barriers are crucial in keeping the interaction fun and how they also help to camouflage the sexual advance. The more silly or outrageous the Sexual Hoop, the more silly and outrageous the false barrier should be. The more serious and real the Sexual Hoop, the more serious the false barrier can be. A good rule of thumb is to use playful reasons, semi-serious reasons or logistical reasons. You will notice in the examples above that the playful false barrier is important to the hoop. Without it, the comment could be too forward and make the text almost creepy. As long as you are in the first few Sexual Hoops, you should keep the barriers light or funny.

Real False Barriers

The most advanced use of False Barriers is when you highlight a potential real barrier. These are hard to find and cannot be forced, but if you can find a real one they are explosive for building sexual tension and deep levels of comfort.

Real False Barriers work on the principle of scarcity. What is the sure fire way to make something valuable? Make it scarce. A Real False Barrier makes things scarce.

The best way to use Real False Barriers is to move through all of the Sexual Hoops and get a woman sexually attracted, turned on, and invested. Shortly thereafter, you incorporate a real barrier for why you cannot act on your mutual attraction and how frustrating it is for both of you.

When you do this properly, you can make a woman go from 'kind of interested' in having sex with you, to making her work hard to have sex with you. Done correctly, Real False Barriers also sub communicate that you have standards, self respect, and high character. This makes Real False Barriers one of the most powerful tools in your arsenal.

Real False Barriers should be introduced at the peak of mutual Sexualization and attraction. The Real False Barrier should set the frame - "I want to sleep with you so bad, but what about... X or Y?" or, "I want to sleep w/ you so bad, it sucks you live in (X city far away)." Or, "I want to sleep with you so bad, what about your friend X?" These are things that place her in the seat of the one attempting to convince you that having sex is ok.

It is crucial that when attempting to incorporate Real False Barriers, you remember the following rules:

- First, make sure that the False Barrier is a barrier that could be overcome. If you make the barrier so real and difficult that she cannot overcome it, you will lose her. For example, a barrier such as, "I want to sleep with you so bad, but I'm married and have two kids" would be quite hard to get over. Even, "I want to sleep with you so bad, but I have a girlfriend" is not a good barrier.

- Second, make sure that the barrier is something that she can psychologically rationalize via loopholes or technicalities. The barrier has to be one that she can overcome with minimal effort, but that requires enough effort to make her see you as a scarce resource that she better act on soon.

- Finally, be careful about throwing up barriers that put her character or self respect on the line. You do not want her to feel the emotion of guilt. You want her to feel compelled to overcome the barrier to get the scarce resource (i.e. you), but you do not want to make the barrier something that calls her character into question. Doing this could kill your chance of having sex with her, instead of being a catalyst to it. For example, "I want to sleep with you so bad, but I don't date girls who sleep with guys too soon" or "I want to sleep with you so bad, but don't you feel bad about stabbing your best friend in the back?" will obviously both work against your chances of sleeping with her.

The following are examples of good Real False Barriers:

Braddock: *"You know I want you too, but we can't. It would kill your friend Jenny." [Note that this is used, when you now for a fact that the girl and Jenny are mere acquaintances at best and that the girl does not care what Jenny thinks.]*

Braddock: *"You know I like you too, but I feel bad because you are kind of dating that Brian guy." [Note that this is used when you know that Brian flirts with her, but that she is hardly interested or obviously more interested in you. This also assumes you are Brian are not close friends.]*

Braddock: *"You know I like you too, but you just got out of a relationship so I need to think about this. I've been there.... we met at a horrible time." [Note that this is used when you know she is clearly over her ex and that she obviously likes you more. Do not use this when the woman is clearly hurt and not sure if she is over the guy. She will quickly agree which would work against you.]*

Braddock: *"I've never been so attracted to someone, but we can't because I don't want to end up liking you." [This should only be used when your value is clearly higher than hers and you can tell that she is worried that you will just sleep with her and never call her.]*

Braddock: *"I've never been so attracted to someone, but maybe we shouldn't because we work together."*

Braddock: *"I like you, but you would be bad for me. I promised myself I wouldn't like anyone for a long time. I'm afraid if I got to know you anymore you would mess that up."*

Braddock: *"I want to sleep with you so bad, but I can't because I think that my friend X likes you" [Note: be careful with this one. While it is powerful, you don't want to do it to a close friend]*

Braddock: *"I want to sleep with you so bad, but what about your friend X?"*

Booty Call Phone and Texting

Booty call texts should be reserved for women that you have zero fear of losing and will not cause repercussions in any important social circle.

These texts are also reserved for women you have already slept with that you set proper frames in person. Setting up a booty call through text from scratch can be tough. This book is focused on Text and Phone Game, so we will only give a brief description of what it takes to turn a woman into a 'friend with benefits.'

If you want to turn a woman into a friend with benefits you are well behind the eight ball if you are waiting until you have her phone number to start steering the relationship in that direction. Ideally you start in the initial interaction, during, or just after sex.

Here are four of strategies which you can use to help create this scenario:

1. Start pushing things in this direction as soon as you know that she is attracted to you and there is a high level of reciprocity with touching. You do this by using Sexual Hoops in conversation. If you can get her all the way to the third hoop, where she is sexually qualifying herself to you, then you can now start setting friends with benefits frames.

2. Run standard game and wait until just before sex to set the same frame that you 'shouldn't' because, while you are really into her and really attracted to her, you are just not looking for a relationship. The key here is to make it clear that you are really attracted to her and that you think that she is amazing, but you do not want a relationship with ANYONE and you will not want a relationship for a long time. If you say this just about her, but you still try to have sex with her, you will likely make her feel bad and she will have a negative response. It is also important to make it clear that you will only be friends with benefits with her. This gives her mind the feeling that this is somewhat special and that you are not using her.

The important frames to set are:

- You do not want a girlfriend and will not want one for a long time.
- She is amazing.
- You are really attracted to her.
- You do not like one night stands and do not like to sleep around, but you like spending time with her.

She will often ask, "Well if you don't want a girlfriend and you don't sleep around, what do you want?" The answer is that you want someone that is

(a) very sexually open,
(b) wants to have sex all the time,
(c) will not get weird, needy and want a relationship and
(d) will not tell anyone.

When you tell a woman this, she will often object on little details. The key is not to try to over explain or sound like you are trying to convince her. Just calmly tell her what you are looking for in a 'matter of fact' tone. If you sound like you are trying to convince her or if you are taking too much heed of her negative reactions, then you will lose her. You have to be strong about what you want without pushing for it or making her feel bad.

It is crucial that once she accepts this, you make it clear exactly what you want and expect out of the relationship. You can do this just before (i.e. during escalation) and even during sex. While doing so, it is also crucial that you frame it as a positive thing. As you are undressing her or as you are having sex, you can sprinkle in the frames that you have already set to make them really stick.

For example, during sex you can say things like:

> **Braddock:** *"I think it's so hot that we can do this and not have strings attached."*

Later on you can reinforce these frames:

> **Braddock:** *"You know what is really hot about this?"*
>
> **Tiffany:** *"What?"*
>
> **Braddock:** *"When we are around our friends, nobody has any clue that we have sex all the time and we will have to play it cool. That's hot. I've never had to do that before."*

Other examples and variations include:

> **Braddock:** *"Wow, it's so hot that we can do this with no strings attached. Why does that make it so much hotter? I love that you are cool with this. Most girls would get weird and ruin a good thing."*
>
> **Braddock:** *"Wow, you are great in bed. I can't believe we get to do this*

all the time without all the relationship drama. That turns me on so much. You know what I mean?"

3. Run standard game and just never mention relationships. You can have sex for weeks or months before she brings it up. When she tries to talk about it, you are vague and tell her that you like what you have and you do not want to complicate things with titles.

This is probably the least effective long term strategy, because it alludes to the idea that she is your girlfriend while just not addressing it. It usually ends with her feelings hurt. The other two strategies do not. This can actually work really well depending on the woman. A lot of women are totally down and need almost zero framing at all. You will not need to ever mention what is going on or how things should be. Just make sure you sleep with them no more than once per week.

4. Run 'asshole game'. This is reserved for women that you are already sleeping with who know the score. They know you only want to have sex with them and they know that no matter what happened you would not care. If she got mad about the situation and walked away, you could care less. The Power Ratio will need to be highly in your favor and you should have a high level of attraction. This style can be risky and come across as rude and abrupt, so please refrain from using this in your social circle or on any woman that you would consider having a relationship with.

The basic premise is 'take it or leave it'. You basically declare your sexual intent and let the chips fall as they may. This does not mean that you go out of your way to be mean to her, it just means that you do not text much unless it's about getting down to business. You basically act like a Long Fuse to her unless you are looking to hook up. She will typically respond in one of two ways - either she will get mad or accept the frame.

Either way, you have to hold the frame that you are not interested unless she wants to have sex (note that you do not have to express this directly but it is the underlying frame or thought). Once she becomes ok with this, be ready for her to do the same thing to you. Sometimes you will invite her over and she will give you one word answers telling you 'no.' Other times she will send you short messages to see if you are down. If you expect her to be cool, you have to be cool and relaxed as well.

If she gets mad and stops replying, then delete the number and move on. If she gets mad but continues to text you and call you, just keep pushing sexually without being mean. Do not be rude or mean, just be blunt.

Friends With Benefits: Putting it All Together:

Here is an example of a real life interaction [not text game] that sets a 'friends with benefits' frame:

Braddock: *[Said while making out]* "*We should stop.*"

Hannah: "*Why?*"

Braddock: "*Because I'm going to try to take your clothes off if we keep going and that would be bad.*"

Hannah: "*Who said I would let you and why would that be bad?*"

Braddock: "*Because you are probably horrible in bed and that would highly disappointing because you are an amazing kisser.*"

Hannah: "*ah…I'm not horrible in bed!*"

Braddock: "*Yeah, but you are so the 'what are we' girl.*"

Hannah: "*What does that mean!?*"

Braddock: "*It means that we would have amazing sex and you would ruin it right after because you are a closed minded Midwestern girl.*"

Hannah: "*HA!!! How would I ruin it jerk? Wow someone is awfully confident… who said I would have sex with you?*"

Braddock: "*We would have amazing sex (at least I would be amazing) and as soon as it was over, you would say… "Listen, since we had sex… What are we? I need to tell my friends and maybe take out a billboard over a major freeway and change our facebook to "in a relationship."*"

Hannah: "*OMG! I'm so not like that! You are so mean. Why would you think that? You must be talking to some weird girls. I would never say that! You are such a player.*"

Braddock: *"Yawwwn… Yep, then you'll be mad at me when you find out I have a wife and 4 kids and then you'll be a crazy home wrecker."*

Hannah: *"God I hate you! You are funny, but I hate you. I like how you avoided the player comment."*

Braddock: *"I'm still going to try to have sex with you even though you are hell bent on ruining a fun thing. (Being as you have an amazing ass that a bird could perch on, it's worth losing you as a friend). I'll just board the windows on my house and park my car in the garage for when you switch to crazy girl mode."*

Hannah: *"HAHAHA You are an asshole! I do have a nice ass huh? I'm not a crazy girl. Who have you been dating? Also, why do you keep assuming I will have sex with you?"*

Braddock: *"Maybe because I deserve it. I've taken you to get a drink and let you meet my friends. Technically after that much effort, you owe me a threesome or something involving a live animal. (Tame and house broken of course). Not to mention I'm the only 25 year old virgin left and I promised all my friends that 2009 would be my year. Clocks ticking… it's November."*

Hannah: *"HAHAHA Who are you? You are crazy. Where do you get this stuff?"*

Hannah: *"P. S. You are no virgin. You are a slut."*

Braddock: *"Most of these lines are from a book I've been reading on how to get a girlfriend. How am I doing so far? Not a virgin? Whatever. I talk a big game, but I bet I'll be sooo awkward in bed my first time. What am I sup pose to do with my hands?"*

Hannah: *"HHAHAHA… I'm pretty sure you don't want a girlfriend jerk. Quit saying you are a virgin."*

Braddock: *"See! I mention one self help book I'm reading and you are already hinting about being my girlfriend! You are soooo going to throw a brick through my window after our threesome."*

Hannah: *"WHATEVER!!!! Lolol You know that's not what I meant. We ARE NOT having a threesome! Quit dropping that in mr."*

Braddock: *"Awww… so you do admit that we are having sex soon. Yee-ees. I so knew you wanted to take my virginity. What did it… the lip ring or my ass like an earthquake?"*

Hannah: *"Ummm… definitely isn't your ass. You have no ass! Must be how sweet and nice you are… o wait."*

Braddock: *"Maybe I would be nicer if you would ever talk about something besides sex. Is that all this is?"*

Hannah: *"HA! Mr. "You're the what are we girl." You are unreal."*

Braddock: *"Fine I'm getting pissed off. Come make out with me and say you are sorry."*

Hannah: *"You are so random."*

Braddock: *"Will you send me a pic I want to show my mom my new girlfriend?"*

Hannah: *"lol. . . . Why should I give you one?"*

Braddock: *"What am I going to give the security guard for when you go crazy?"*

Hannah: *"LOL… How did I not see that one coming."*

Here are a few other important rules which apply to a 'friends with benefits' relationship:

- Make sure that you only have sex or even spend exclusive time with her once a week (twice at maximum). If you hang out anymore than that, you will be crossing the threshold into a relationship.

- Do not say things or do activities that would signal to her that you are in a relationship. If you take her to expensive dinners and tell her how special she is, you are no longer friends with benefits. The best thing to do is be really flirty and playful all the time, without being romantic. Romance is reserved for women that you want to date. She should feel respected, she should feel like you are glad that she is there and she should feel like you cannot keep your hands off of her. But she should not feel like you want to have her as an exclusive girlfriend.

One way to avoid this is by limiting the time that you allow her to linger the morning after sleeping together. If she stays until noon and you watch movies in bed, then you are flipping the relationship switch. However, if you make her feel like she was kicked out, you will make her feel disrespected. The happy medium is to either
(a) have sex at her house and make sure you leave in the morning under the pretense that you have to work/handle some responsibility
or
(b) have sex at your house, but the night before, set your alarm right in front of her so it is blatantly clear that you have something to do in the morning. When you wake up in the morning, wake her up too. Do not let her stay in your house while you are gone.

What if you do not have anything to do because it's Saturday? Pretend that you have something to do, set the alarm clock, get up, get dressed, drive the car around the block and drop her off, come back home and go to bed. That may sound bad, but it is a necessary evil if you want to maintain the friends with benefits scenario and not let it slip into a 'relationship' frame.

- Realize that as soon as she gets too attached and she no longer has fun knowing that she is having sex, but can not have you as a boyfriend, she will cut off the sexual relationship so she will not feel bad anymore. The key is to keep her interested without letting her get so attached that the fun and attraction turns to pain and jealousy. This can be difficult to do and you will most likely get it wrong a few times, but it is possible.

How To Text Friends With Benefits: The Art Of The Booty Call Text

Just about any woman will be friends with benefits with the right guy. Most guys miss their chance of achieving friends with benefits by not respecting each woman's blueprint. They try to run the same exact game on each woman regardless of whether she is responding.

Each type of woman will want to be treated slightly differently and will respond better to certain types of dialogue. Some women know it's not a relationship, but want some of the pieces of a relationship. Some women are fine with it being straight business. Other women will do it as long as they think you might be there boyfriend someday. You will only be able to recognize the optimal text to use through experience with her.

One important mistake to avoid is assuming that you need to go all the way through the Sexual Hoops each time you want a booty call to come over. This could not be farther from the truth. Once you have already had sex, you do not need to push the Sexual Hoops each time. They know exactly what's going on, so you simply need to get her over. As a matter of fact, talking dirty can actually kill it because it makes it to real. On some level, she likes the idea that you two are "just going to watch a movie."

Using your Callback Humor and role plays can be helpful here, but as an example here are some that we like to use:

- **Braddock:** *"Bible study…my house…tonight."*

- **Braddock:** *"What are you doing sexy? I want to see you tonight."*

- **Braddock:** *"Movie at my house tonight or we are breaking up for good."*

- **Braddock:** *"We should probably have sex later."*

- **Braddock:** *"I wanna see you, come watch a movie with me."*

- **Braddock:** *"I'm coming over and sleeping in your bed tonight, you are welcome to join if you want."*

- **Mr M:** *"Get out of my head and get over here."*

- **Mr M:** *"I want to do bad things to you tonight"*

Sexualization on the Phone

All of the principles, techniques and rules above apply to Sexualization on the phone. Sexual Hoops, Baiting and mirroring intent, Power Ratio, False Barriers, etc can all be applied on the phone with even greater efficacy than they can be over text message. However, since phone conversation gives you a lot less time to think about your response than text messaging, practicing the above techniques initially via texts, can greatly increase your Calibration on the phone.

The 4 Main Factors to Consider When Going Sexual

1. Fuse Length. For each fuse length we will have a slightly different strategy.

2. Power Ratio. Going sexual on a woman where you have a low Power Ratio is a bad idea.

3. Responsiveness to sexual baiting. What happens when you try to bait her sexually?
- If she takes the bait, then you are on the right track.
- If she does not take the bait, or gives you a negative response, then back off and save Sexualization for when her comfort level has increased.

4. How much sexual dialogue (or lack thereof), has taken place so far:
- If you did not take things sexual at all when you met, you will need to ease into Sexualization through baiting. Going extremely sexual right away through text or on the phone will seem weird.
- If you had a high level of sexual dialogue when you met, you should still bait, but it is much more likely that you can escalate faster and further.

Sexualization Do's and Don'ts:
Do's

1. Do switch between sexual conversation and humor and normal conversation.
2. Do try to misinterpret her texts in a sexual way every once in a while.
3. Do incorporate funny sexual stories (not about you) and jokes to gauge her reaction.
4. Do continuously adjust your speed of escalation based on her feedback.
5. Do allude to things you want to do to her, but do not name them outright, unless you have already slept with her or are dating her.
6. Do test how sexual she can be slowly. Going too sexual too quick puts you at a high risk of losing her.
7. Do maintain a playful and flirty air.
8. When you go sexual, try to stay challenging. Do not give full rapport. Challenge her.
9. Do realize that just because you had sex with a girl does not mean that you can talk dirty to her any time (although this does make it easier).

Don'ts

1. Don't go sexual until you have a decent level of investment.
2. Don't try to be sexual all the time.
3. Don't try to go sexual to early on unless you baited her into it and she ran with it first.
4. Don't misinterpret every text as sexual. You will simply turn out looking like a horny 7th grader.
5. Don't try to get her to commit to an actual sexual act. Stay vague and dance around the topic .
6. If you take things too far, do not say, "I'm sorry". Merely ignore it, allow an adequate amount of time to pass, and text her something normal later.
7. Do not come off sexually needy. This will creep girls out, turn them off, and maybe even scare them. If you were sexually baiting them properly, this would not be an issue.

Key Points of this Chapter

- There are large benefits of learning to properly sexualize your Text and Phone Game. However, keep in mind that you can also destroy an encounter by sexualizing a conversation improperly.

- Only take things sexual when the Power Ratio is in your favor. The Power Ratio is determined by who has the most attraction, Tempo and emotional pull.

- The shorter the fuse, the higher the Power Ratio and the more likely it is that she will be willing to go sexual with you.

- Test her comfort levels by sexually baiting to see how she responds. A good rule is to bait and then mirror her sexual intent or playfulness.

- Sexual Hoops are a powerful tool which can be used to make conversations sexual. The idea is to introduce small hoops at first and gradually work up to larger and larger hoops. Each sexual hoop that she agrees to, or plays along with, builds sexual receptivity and compliance.
- False barriers are real or playful reasons why you both cannot act on your sexual intent or attraction. Having a barrier to hooking up is a powerful way to build sexual tension.

CHAPTER 9: MEET UP STRATEGIES

IN THIS CHAPTER:

- A Few Common Mistakes

- The Basic Structure of Going for the Meet Up

- The Distracter Technique (credit DaHunter)

- Meet Up Strategies Based on Fuse Length

Chapter 9 - Meet Up Strategies

Up to this point, we have covered all kinds of different strategies and scenarios for how to use your texts and phone calls to pique a woman's interest, build her attraction, comfort and investment and keep things moving toward the date. Now we will explore exactly how to ask her out.

This chapter builds on previous chapters. If you find that you do not understand some of the key terms and ideas that appear in this chapter, please go back and revisit the previous chapters.

A Few Common Mistakes

Before we cover the tactical side of asking the woman out, here are some basic rules that you should follow to increase your success rate.

Avoid Making the Meet up a Formal Process

One of the most common mistakes is when men set up the second meeting like they would set up a business meeting. This typically creates an awkward 'professional' or formal vibe to the meet up which either makes the woman nervous about seeing him and flake, or leads to an awkward first date. The key to avoiding this is to adopt the mindset that she should want to spend time with you because you would both likely have a lot of fun out together. When you adopt this mindset you tend to ask her out with a lot more confidence.

Another way that guys make meeting up feel like a formal process for a woman is by going for the invite right out of the gate. Do not be tempted to do this. Executed correctly, the invite should be more of a side note to the conversation and flow so seamlessly that she almost did not notice it.

Suggest a Meet Up at a High Point in the Conversation

Ideally, suggest a meet up at a high point in the conversation. A 'high point' means when she is laughing, seems really into the interaction and when you have Tempo. Remember - women are emotional creatures who act in the moment. Consequently, if she is in a good state when you ask her out, you are much more likely to get a positive response. One of the biggest mistakes that you can make is waiting to ask to meet up when the conversation has passed its peak and is running out of steam. While you cannot always time things perfectly, ideally you want to ask her out just at the crest of a great conversation.

For example, let's say you have both been enthusiastically laughing and talking up to this point, you could say something like

> *"Hey, I gotta get back to work, but are you free Thursday?"*

TIP: Think of a phone call where you ask a woman out like a roller coaster. You want to extend the invite as the roller coaster is climbing up the hill (or is ideally at the top of the hill), rather than when it is at a low point.

Do Not 'Over Game'

You should do the least amount of work possible to get her on a date.

Many guys make the mistake of 'over gaming'. This means that they had the woman completely into them, and she would have agreed to go on a date if they would have sent a short text inviting her or called her and simply asked her out. Instead, many guys try to be overly hard, distant, funny or creative. The more value that you have in the woman's eyes, the less creative you will need to be with your invites. The less value that you have in the woman's eyes, the more work you will have to do. This is why many social circle hookups require nothing more than a simple phone call.

The Basic Structure of Going for the Meet Up

Before going through each fuse length, we are going to cover the basic structure that you can use every time when going
for the meet up. Here is the formula:

1. If this is the first time that you have called her, then you can begin the conversation with, the line 'What are you doing? ' This conveys immediate comfort. As an example:

   Natasha: "Hello?"

   Mr M: "Hey. How's it going?"

   Natasha: "Good thanks."

   Mr M: "What you doing?"

2. Jump immediately into Callback Humor or including her in on a funny story or relate something about your day.
   For example:

   Natasha: "I'm just watching TV."

   Mr M: "You couch potato. Have you fed our kids?" [Callback Humor]

   Natasha: "Haha… no, they are downstairs crying."

   Mr M: "Listen, this just isn't working out. I'm taking the kids and going to stay at your sister's place until you get yourself sorted out and clean."

   Natasha: "Haha… ok I'll be here drinking whisky."

   Mr M: "I was at a bar today and there were these Russians. You said you speak Russian right?"

   Natasha: "Yeah…"

   Mr M: "Well, they started getting pretty wasted and then had an argument with the bartender. Security came over and were like physically restraining them but they didn't know how to speak English and the bartenders didn't know how to speak Russian. Some of them didn't even know what was going on. We needed a translator. Where were you?"

   Natasha: "Haha… probably at home sleeping."

   Mr M: "Well, you need to be out there saving crazy Russians."

Natasha: "Haha…"

3. Ask her questions or make statements about things going on in her day.

   Mr M: "Hey, did you say you sing?" [She mentioned singing]

   Natasha: "No. I said that I wanted to be a singer when I was younger."

   Mr M: "Oh. Well you can still live your dreams at the local karaoke bar. I've got a good visual."

   Natasha: "Haha… no! It's been a long time since I've been to karaoke."

   Mr M: "Do you sing in the shower?"

   Natasha: "No."

   Mr M: "It's good practice. In fact, statistics show that 95% of people sing in the shower and 5% masturbate. Do you know what they sing?"

   Natasha: "No."

   Mr M: "Then you must be one of the 5%."

   Natasha: "Haha!"

   Mr M: "What you up to today?"

   Natasha: "Not much, probably just doing some groceries."

   Mr M: "Cool. I love grocery shopping. Can I ride in the shopping trolley?"

   Natasha: "Haha… no!"

   Mr M: "When I was younger I used to ride shopping trolleys in the car park while my mum went shopping. One day, I hit this limited edition Aston Martin while the owner was still in the car."

   Natasha: "No way!"

Mr M: *"Yes way."*

Natasha: *"What happened?"*

Mr M: *"He got out and chased me but I ran inside the Wal Mart and hid next to the toothbrush section. To this day I feel a sense of security every time I pick up my toothbrush."*

Natasha: *"Haha! You're crazy!"*

4. On a high note, get down to business and ask for the meet up. Keep the invite casual and low pressure, meaning something that is not overly romantic or time consuming.

   Mr M: *"Hey, my friend is here and I can't stay for much longer. I don't have my schedule on me but I think I'm busy on Friday and Saturday but I'm free Thursday. You wanna grab a drink?"*

   Natasha: *"Umm let me see… I can't on Thursday."*

   Mr M: *"I'm free after 7pm on Wednesday. You wanna do that instead?"*
   [Note: if she said "no" at this point, Mr M simply would have said that he would call or text her again in future, but as a general rule, do not ask for a meet up more than twice]

   Natasha: *"Sure, that sounds good."*

5. Change the subject after organizing the meet up and look to be the first to have to leave the conversation when it is on a high note.

   Mr M: *"By the way, you know that guy who was being all weird and creepy at [the bar you met at]. Did you think he looked like [name of famous person]?"*

   Natasha: *"Sort of… yeah!"*

   The conversation continues until you leave on a high point. You can either give her specific details about where to meet you or tell her that you will text her the exact details and do it immediately after the phone call.

Our experience has shown that when you are asking for the woman to meet you again, calling her to meet up highly reduces flaking. However, if you are going to ask her out via text, a creative/funny line that you can use to reduce flaking is something like:

"LETS MEET AT [INSERT PLACE]. TEXT '1' FOR YES AND '2' FOR DEFINITELY".

Below are two further examples of phone calls instigating a meet up. One is an example of a bad phone call, while the other is an example of a good phone call. The situation is as follows. Braddock is dealing with a Medium Fuse and he has done everything correctly leading up to this phone call. He ran good game when they met, number closed her properly by making sure that she saved his number in her phone, and he has been texting her and utilizing Callback Humor from when they met. She has been texting him back and he can tell that it is time to call her and ask her out as she is becoming a Short Fuse.

Example of a Bad Phone Call:

Britney: "Hello."

Braddock: "Hey Britney, what's up?"

Britney: "Not much."

Braddock: "That's cool. Did you have to work today?"

Britney: "Yeah. I just got off."

Braddock: "How was that?"

Britney: "It was ok. I didn't have that much to do."

Braddock: "You said you work at a clothing store down on Melrose, right?"

Britney: "Yep."

Braddock: "Yeah, I thought that's what you told me. So, what are you doing now?"

Britney: "I'm about to go to yoga class with my friend."

Braddock: "I hear yoga is really hard. Do you like it?"

Britney: "Yep, it's cool. Hey, listen I'm actually about to walk into the gym so I have to let you go."

Braddock: "Ok, no problem. Real quick, the reason I called was to see if you wanted to grab a drink tonight?"

Britney: [Insert lame excuse]

Example of a Good Phone Call:

Britney: "Hello."

Braddock: "Hi, I'm standing in the bathroom of the Chevron gas station and on the wall it says for a good time to call this number and ask for Britney."

Britney: "Haha… is that so? I called them and told them to erase that, I can't believe it's still up."

Braddock: "Haha… yeah, for sure. That's really disappointing. So did you catch anyone stealing any clothes to day?"

Britney: "Haha… no but I did have this annoying girl come in and try on like 300 pairs of jeans and not buy any of them. It took me like an hour to put them all back. I hate that!"

Braddock: "I don't know if they told you this or not when you applied at that clothing store, but when people go clothes shopping they usually try stuff on."

Britney: "Smart ass! This went well beyond trying stuff on. It looked like a tornado hit the store when she left."

Braddock: "Haha… that would suck."

Britney: "What are you doing, Oklahoma boy?"

Braddock: *"Well I met this really cute girl that works in this clothing store on Melrose and I wanted to see if she wanted to get a drink with me later this week, but I'm not sure how to ask her. I mean she is like really pushy and intimidating when she was trying to sell me stuff, so I have no idea how she will be on the phone. She will probably try to up sell me from a drink, to dinner, to a weekend in France. Any advice on how I should ask her?"*

Britney: *"Haha... I was not pushy when you were in my store!"*

Braddock: *"She was so pushy I almost asked to see the manager."*

Britney: *"Haha... whatever! If she was that pushy, maybe you shouldn't ask her for a drink."*

Braddock: *"Yeah, but she was really cute and I want to score a discount someday. I was thinking about asking her out for Wednesday night. What do you think, is that a good night to ask her out?"*

Britney: *"Haha... that's probably fine. Are you going to be a smart ass like this on your date with her?"*

Braddock: *"I'm from Oklahoma, I would never be a smart ass. I'm all about romance and being a gentleman. I was even going to pick her up in a limo and have diamonds and flowers waiting."*

Britney: *"Haha... yeah right. Well, I'm walking into Yoga class so I have to run, but when should I expect the limo?"*

Braddock: *"I will send the driver to pick you up at 8pm on Wednesday."*

Britney: *"Ha... sounds good."*

Braddock: *"Alright, talk to you Wednesday sucka."*

Britney: *"Ok, bye Oklahoma boy."*

Braddock: *"Bye."*

The Distracter Technique (credit DaHunter)

The Distracter Technique states that you should always say something funny when you ask a woman out via phone or text message to distract her from the intent and to lessen the impact of asking her out. It is a good general rule of thumb and is described in Love System Instructor DaHunter's classic post on the Distracter Technique on the following page:

Distractor
By DaHunter, Love Systems Instructor

This is a technique that I use whenever I want to ask a girl out. The fact that you want something from her (i.e. to meet up with her) will automatically sub communicate lower value. To solve this problem, you can use 'Distractors' whenever you want to get something from a girl. This is particularly something I use in phone game and text messages. So let's say your goal is to get her to come out with you. The average guy will say:

"Hey let's go out"
"We should hang out"
"Come with me to X"

The thing is, these are all correct, except that you need to add a Distractor afterwards. No girl wants to say "yes" without adding more to the sentence because it will make her feel uncomfortable (which is bad comfort game). Further, adding humor takes the edge off of the invite. So instead we want to say things like:

"Hey let's go out, but you gotta buy me a present, I'm high maintenance"
"We should hang out, I'm at the gym right now so I can only hang out after 8"
"Come with me to X, just so you know if you're friends with me you have to love white wine, otherwise we wouldn't
be able to hang out"

This Distractor takes the pressure off the "yes". To add to this, she can even deny the Distractor and say something like "Oh no I'm not buying you a present, I'm broke". The power of this is that she can still say "no" to something in the sentence and say "yes" to the real purpose.

It is the same way that in standard game theory, when you say something like "I like you", it can make a girl uncomfortable, which is why you add "too bad you're such a dork" to it. It lessens the blow and it becomes easier for her to respond because it's not overly serious or heavy. Remember, we want to stay away from heavy vibes and be playful.

(Adapted from: http//www.theattractionforums.com/dahunter/54277-distractor.html)

Meet Up Strategies Based on Fuse Length

Short Fuse

With a Short Fuse, you can get away with just about anything. It is even an option to invite her out using text alone. While it is suggested you make the phone call, you can definitely achieve a high level of success by simply using text with Short Fuses. For example:

> **Braddock:** *"What up brat? How's your day?"*
>
> **Jenny:** *"Hey you! My day has been fantastic. How is yours sexy?"*
>
> **Braddock:** *"My day is awesome sauce. Let's grab a drink later."*

Another example:

> This interaction occurred after Braddock and Jessica had been texting back and forth for a number of days, after which she became a Short Fuse.
>
> **Braddock:** *"Hi, Jessica Smith ;)"*
>
> **Jessica:** *"Hi, Braddock… Are you having fun in my city?"*
>
> **Braddock:** *"The food and weather sucks, but I met this really cute blonde girl named Jessica a few days ago. Pretty excited about her."*
> Jessica: *"Oh yeah, tell me more?"*
>
> **Braddock:** *"Can't remember much, but she was pretty fun, works at Northern Realty and hates cats. Let's grab a drink tonight and I'll tell you all about her ;)"*
>
> **Jessica:** *"Lol. OK, where and when cutie?"*

Medium and Long Fuses

A Medium to Long Fuse is unlikely to come out on a 1-1 date with you. With Long Fuses in particular, the best strategy is to avoid asking for dates until they become at least Medium Fueses and ideally Short Fuses. The two best ways to convert a Medium or Long Fuse into a date are:

1. Getting them to become Short Fuses first by using Tempo, and building attraction, comfort and value prior to asking her on the date. How to do this is covered comprehensively in earlier chapters.

2. Try to get her out in person by using any of the following techniques:

- Extend a "You guys should meet us out" invite.

- Send her what appears to be a bulk text inviting everyone to an event.

- Let her know about a special event where you have situational value (for example, if you and any of your friends are playing in a band, acting, going to somewhere exclusive, etc).

- If she is part of your social circle, invite friends around her who may be closer to you and can bring her along.

The key strategy is that you see her out with you again and build your value quickly.

For many guys who are good at meeting women and dating, chasing a Long Fuse and putting in the additional effort for a meet up may not seem worthwhile, unless she is extremely attractive or a good social connector. This is because once you get good at Love Systems, it should be very easy to meet women and get plenty of phone numbers at least on a Medium Fuse (or better) basis.

Above all, maintain an abundance mindset in you Text and Phone Game and always focus on overall improvement rather than any one woman.

Key Points of this Chapter

- Avoid making the meet up a formal process.

- Suggest a meet up at a high point in the conversation. If she is in a good state when you ask her out, you are much more likely to get a positive response.

- Do not 'over game'. Do the least amount of work possible to get her on a date.

- The Distractor technique states that you should always say something funny when you ask a woman out via phone or text message. You do this to distract her from the intent and lessen the impact of asking her out.

- The Basic Structure of Going for the Meet Up is:
(1) Call her and immediately use or tell her a funny or interesting story or a story about your day
(2) Ask her questions or make statements about things going on in her day
(3) Suggest the meet up on a high note and remember to keep the invitation casual and low pressure
(4) Change the subject after organizing the meet up and look to be the first to have to leave the conversation when it is at a high point.

CHAPTER 10 : Situations and Scenarios

Chapter 10 - Situations and Scenarios

What should you do if a woman does not call you back?

Some women are just busy, distracted or have strange ideas about the appropriateness of calling men. They may even be deliberately screening for men who are persistent. Unless she is going to tell other people with whom you're likely to interact that you are a creep (this is most dangerous in a social circle situation), it is okay to call or text a few times to try to make contact. You never know what is going on in her head. However, follow the rules of Long Fuses here and do not seem needy by calling or texting more than once a day. If you call twice in one day, try calling her in 2 days. You do not want to come across as needy under any circumstances. Neediness causes death in attraction.

It is also important to adopt a solid frame, to yourself, that she is just a flaky woman and that it is kind of cute. Do not let it play in your mind that she might not actually be interested in you. This is an unproductive thought.

If she does not call back, don't acknowledge it. Do not ever say "this is the last time I'm calling" or "I'm calling to leave you another message". If you do get her on the phone, do not bring up the subject of your previous calls/texts as this will signal to her that you have been thinking about it a lot, which will most likely lower your value.

> **Indicators of Low Compliance**
>
> The following indicates that a woman's compliance is low:
>
> - She gives excessively short answers every time.
>
> - She gives excessively formal answers to texts that are laden with jokes.
>
> - She stops replying completely.
>
> - She only replies to every third text or more.
>
> - She takes hours or days to reply every time and even then the answers are weak attempts to address the content of your text.
>
> - She disqualifies herself a lot. (i.e. she gives the opposite answer of what she thinks you want to hear to questions or to jokes).
>
> - She replies with rude messages.

If she doesn't call back, simply leave it a couple of days and then try calling again.
There are a number of practical steps that you can take to re-ignite

contact:

- **Method of contact** – Switching the method of contact can encourage a response. Low investment text messages can work well here. You can also try calling from a different number, such as your work phone or landline. Do not block your phone number when you call her. Many girls will not answer a call from a withheld number, so you may encourage her not to answer.

- **Time of day** – Many girls are genuinely busy so try varying the time of day when you call – morning, afternoon, evening and night. If you are getting nowhere and want to try a Hail Mary, try calling after midnight. You will probably wake her up, so make sure you can be immediately entertaining from the second she answers. Start with a high-energy, funny, short routine and do not even introduce yourself.

- **Special occasions** – Do not delete numbers that flake. You can keep these numbers around and 'reawaken' them in future. Holidays can be a great occasion for women to come out of the woodwork on your phone. Texting every woman in your phone book with "Happy New Year" or "Merry Xmas" or "Happy Easter" can sometimes help reconnect you with a couple of them.

- **In case of emergencies** – When all else fails, you can try texting her "I just met your twin". This may not only jar her into responding, but to responding with a competitive frame. Often her response will be "is she prettier than me?" or "I'm cooler". Save this till you have exhausted all other avenues.

What to do if investment is very low?

Low investment can happen for many reasons. Your value can come and go quickly and is often more dependent on her circumstances than your 'game'. This is why cold approach can be challenging.

It is important to understand that low investment women will do none of the work for you. If you do not build attraction or comfort with them when you first meet, then you can count on them putting in very little effort to help you bridge that gap in the near future.

Because there are so many factors that cause low investment, it is not worth you spending much time and mental energy analyzing why. While it is crucial that you look for patterns and become self correcting, beating yourself up or over analyzing every time a woman flakes or becomes low investment is unhealthy and illogical. However, if you are losing girls at the same place each time, then simply take note of this reoccurring theme and focus on making the necessary corrections to avoid it in the future. The following are strategies for dealing with low investment:

- Do not chase. Oftentimes, when guys feel a girl slipping through their fingers, they make the fatal mistake of trying to reel her back by texting more and/or longer texts. Do not ever text from the frame: "I need to correct my mistake." This does not cause her to become more attracted to you. In fact, the opposite is actually true – your neediness causes her to become less attracted to you.

    If you feel that you are beginning to trigger negative responses from her, then you must gain control of your emotions. Force yourself to listen to your logical mind and not allow your emotions to dictate your actions. Even though your brain is telling you to send her something amazingly funny or interesting, realize that there is no perfect line. Anything you send in a situation where you have lost Tempo will only set you back even further. (Note that this rule does not apply to already established relationships).

- **Stop the bleeding.** It's time to stop the bleeding and stop losing value. How? Simply stop communicating with her for a while. This action will most likely give you a clean slate for later. If it was a minor mistake that caused the loss in Tempo or low investment, than simply stop texting her for a day or two and give her time to forget about it. Then send her something light and amusing in a few days and pretend like it never happened.

    Above all, avoid texting her to ask if you have messed up. This creates a lot of social pressure, makes you look needy and any answer you get will not likely give you any genuine feedback. Apologizing for assumed mistakes lowers your value significantly so be extremely careful about this. Also, trying to be overly funny or saying "just kidding" incessantly is emotional overreaching and should be avoided at all costs.

- **Time heals all.** You want to use time to allow any negative associations that were developing to wash away. To determine how much time you need to leave between interactions, ask yourself what caused the shift in attitude.
- If it was a minor infraction and you caught the mistake early enough, than you will need less time before you reinitiate. If it was a major

infraction while investment was already low, then you will need a fair amount of time.

- Machine gun out of ammo? Go to your side arm! If you are fairly certain that you lost her because you ran poor text message game, wait a set amount of time and just call her. There are 3 general instances when you should call a girl:

1. **When investment is very high.** If investment is high than there is only one direction for it to go… DOWN! If she is highly invested and you are certain that you could call her and/or set up the meet, than do so immediately.

   TIP: *While compliance is extremely high, it's not advantageous to push the envelope until you have had sex or at least until you have spent an extensive amount of time together.*

2. **When investment is very low.** If you get little or no investment after several texts, than you should wait a set amount of time and just call her. This is somewhat of a Hail Mary strategy, but at this point, you might as well try.

3. **When investment was extremely high and then it suddenly started to shift in a negative way.** If your text messages are causing more harm than good and killing high investment, then abort the text game. Wait a set amount of time (no more than a few days) and then call her to reinitiate.

What to do if investment is very high?

If investment is very high then you should instantly schedule the meet up through phone call or text. If you have high investment, it is also likely to be the correct time to increase baiting her with more sexually charged themes. However, do not push the envelope too far. A woman who is highly invested is already likely to sleep with you. Consequently, you should err on the side of caution and mainly use 'play it safe' attraction spikes and tactics until you meet for a second time.

Try to continually maintain Tempo when investment is high. You can refer to the Chapter 7 on Value for more on Tempo, however, one way to maintain the upper hand is to avoid being predictable with your responses. To avoid being predictable, do not always send long replies, do not always reply quickly, and do not always be funny. Varying how and when you reply helps build value and scarcity. It will make her feel like she has to earn you. Be careful here though and do not ruin a good situation by playing too many games.

Also note that you have much more leeway for the terms of the meet up when investment is high. When investment is low or medium you often extend a, "you guys should meet us out" type of invite. These invites help maintain as much value as possible in the event she rejects the offer. This is because you were already going, irrespective of her "yes" or "no" response. When investment is high, you can skip this and make a call or send a text where you specifically ask her out on a date.

What if she is sending mixed signals? i.e. 'She flirts but I don't know where I stand!'

Here are some useful points and strategies that are relevant when she is sending mixed signals:

- Mirror her level of investment and do not to exceed them, as this will seem needy.

- Deliberately send mixed signals, while still pushing for a meet up.

- Make sure you are short and succinct, while still flirty.

- Avoid over reaching with too much humor or sending extremely long text messages. Your texts should mirror hers in length and playfulness. Although it is difficult to get this exactly right as you cannot physically see her thoughts or feelings, it is ok to be slightly off. Just ensure that you are not a lot more playful or humorous than she is.

- She may set you up for failure by sending you a fake indication of interest. This is usually a test of the congruence of your frame. If you flinch and take the bait, then it's a major setback. For example, she may directly or indirectly imply that she has strong feelings towards you or misses you. If this is a major jump in tone and out of sync with her other texts, then it is safe to assume that you are being baited. Hold your frame and continue to push for a meet while being short, succinct and still flirty.

What to do if it was on, but it's gone cold: texting to get back in the game!

Do not delete your old numbers. Oftentimes, men make the mistake of deleting old numbers because the woman did not reply after one text, stopped replying after a while, or any number of reasons communication ceased. Unless she flat out says, "don't text/call me anymore", do not delete the number. Simply change your strategy and lower your expectations. This is a similar strategy to what you would do with a Long Fuse.

Women may come in and out of your life after weeks, months, and even years. Oftentimes, they get boyfriends and just cut communication off with all the other men in their life. When that relationship ends, a well timed text message will get you back in the game. This is why mastering the art of low investment texting is so crucial.

This low investment text strategy is applicable in a number of instances and is the foundation of what we call 'Slow Burn Game'. It does not matter how much time has passed (i.e. weeks, months, years). The key is that you make contact by Pinging.

How long should you wait before sending a recovery text? With numbers from cold approach, allow some time, but not too much, because they are more likely to forget who you are. As a general rule, wait a few days if you have texted more than twice in a row and have received no response.

What to text?

If you are not sure what to text, always default to light, non-needy call back humor. Below is a short list of possible text categories for what you can Ping a woman with when you have low investment.

1. Non-needy humor in the form of a statement. For example:

   Braddock: *"Tequila 4. Braddock 0. I would kill a small child for a Tylenol."*

   Braddock: *"It's not completely gay that we haven't hung out this week, but it's definitely pretty gay."*

   Braddock: *"Just wanted to let you know that the new and improved*

Braddock is 23% more awesome."

Braddock: *"Mexican food place on Sunset and Le Brea = Better than sex."*

Braddock: *"Group sex at my house. You bring the girls, I'll make sure Braddock is there."*

Braddock: *"You should come over later for pizza and sex."*
Girl: *"Haha... I don't think so!"*
Braddock: *"What, you don't like pizza?"*

Braddock: *"I having surgery today, pray for me!"*
Girl: *"OMG...on what!??!?"*
Braddock: *"I'm having my awesomeness level reduced by 3%"*

Braddock: *"I'm in Boston and I swear to God there is a girl in here that looks just like you!"*
Girl: *"Really no way!!"*
Braddock: *"Ok, I'm going to go hit on your clone. What would you say to you, if you were going to hit on you?"*

2. Non-needy humor in the form of a short question. For example:

Mr. M: *"Look up! Can you see a cloud that looks like a laughing koala from where you are?"*

Braddock: *"Kim! If we don't hang out soon I'm breaking up with you for real this time. I'm changing my relationship status on facebook and everything. :)"*

Braddock: *"Heading to the gym... Need to build big muscles to overcompensate for small penis. Any other ideas?"*

Braddock: *"Hey, can you help me out?"*
Girl: *"Help you with what?"*
Braddock: *"I want to meet up with this cute girl named [Her name], but she's impossible to nail down. Any advice? Keep in mind she's a total player."*

3. Inside jokes from the past. For example:

Braddock: *"Little Johnny called me and said he was lost. Some mother you are… if you lose him, I'm filing for divorce and I want everything."*

Braddock: *"Make sure the kids have done their homework and dinner is on the table. I've had a long day at work and don't need any more stress."*

Braddock: *"See if your mother will watch the kids tonight. I think we need some alone time."*

4. Intrigue texts that do not ask anything specific, but make her want to reply. For example:

    Braddock: *"I met someone who said they knew you today."*

    Braddock: *"Guess what…"*

    Braddock: *"You are not going to believe what happened to me today."*

5. Pull heart strings. For example:

    Braddock: *"Just heard that Incubus song we used to always play….made me think of you :)"*

    Braddock: *"Just drove through B town… I figured the water tower would say "Home of Sara." :) Hope you are doing well."*

    Braddock: *"X movie is on……made me think of you." [Only use this if there was a connection between the movie and the both of you]*

Note that these usually need to be specific to the woman. These can get really deep if the memory was strong enough and she liked you a lot. However, they should be used sparingly. Using them more than a few times a YEAR will kill your chances with her.

6. Playing a funny false role and pretending that's why you guys have not talked. For example:

    Braddock: *"Did you join the peace corp or something?! I haven't seen you in forever…..I need some Kim in my life!"*

    Braddock: *"Us not talking for 2 months is going beyond playing hard* *to get. You're going to drive me into the arms of several other women at this rate."*

Braddock: *"Did you join The Marines or something? It's been ages! Come spoon me. That's an order."*

7. Just jumping right into a wacky role play. For example:

    Braddock: *"Hi Kim!! Are we broken up for good? You don't, write, you never call, the kids are worried sick and rent was due 6 days ago!"*

    Braddock: *"You never write, you never call, rent's due and the kids are worried sick. What should I tell them?"*

8. Mass texting something funny. For example:

    Mr M: *"April 11, party at Movida. Kssshht, I repeat, the crisps are raiding the liquor store. Mother goose, over …"*

    Braddock: *"Just wanted to remind everyone that I'm cooler than the other side of the pillow. Tell your friends"*

    Braddock: *"Hey all, Mike's farewell party at X bar Friday night. Your mission if you choose to accept it is to show up between the hours of 11pm and 2am. This message will self destruct in 30 sec! Hope to see you there…."*

    Braddock: *"I am 11% more awesome today… that is all."*

    Braddock: *"Hey everyone, don't forget Kev's bday = our house tonight… swim suits = optional… arm floaties = required… safety first ;)"*

Mass texting is a great way to reinitiate old numbers and to ping with a bunch of girls at the same time. Once you send out a mass text, if a girl responds, then you should start building value and using call back humor to build attraction again.

What happens if you did not get far into the initial interaction but you get on the phone with her somehow?

Even if you did not get into comfort in the initial interaction, but managed to get her phone number anyway, you may find that she answers the phone when you call (yes, it does happen - although not with a lot of regularity). If you get into this situation, you basically need to go through a mini Emotional Progression Model. This means that you need to build attraction, qualify her and will probably also need to have a few more calls and text messages in order to build comfort before the actual meet up.

One tactic that you can use if you are stuck in phone game is to make plans with her, even if you know that there is no way that she is going to show up, and then cancel them. The key is that the plans can be tentative, but the cancellation has to be specific. So, for example, saying "we should go to this concert next Friday, I'll call you next week about it" is unlikely to rejected by most women. Next Friday is still likely an abstract concept to her but she likes having many social options for a given night. Saying "yes" to this spares her the social awkwardness of having to say "no".

When the time comes, of course, she will probably not answer your call, or send you a text message that she "has to work" or "isn't feeling well" or "has to pick up her sister at the airport". But for now, she said "yes". The tactic is to treat this as rock-solid and formal plan but then to cancel on her before she can cancel on you. For example, call her the night before or the day of and explain, to her voicemail if you have to, that you can't make it. For example, say that your friend Alexandra is flying out the next day and you totally forgot, but you're hosting a party for her. Further, do not offer to reschedule. This sets a non needy frame that you can build from.

Other Scenarios

Texting girls in other cities or far away

When dealing with girls in other cities, run the Text and Phone Game that has been prescribed in this book up to the point of the phone call. As there will be considerable gaps between the times when you can physically meet up, you should try to run deeper comfort game once you are on the phone with her. This will hopefully hook her hard early on.
The distance issue can sober her up to the reality of how little you can, and actually will, see each other. She may start to question what she is doing and get frustrated and bored. Consequently, once she is hooked and you have a high degree of comfort with her, frame the distance issue as more of a mutual enemy you both hate for keeping you from seeing each other. Remember – natural barriers can amplify attraction. You can also

push the envelope more on attraction, sexual baiting and deeper comfort over phone and text message than you can on a 'local' girl. The fact that you are not likely to interact with anyone in her social circle is a bonus here. It means that she feels less social pressure and is more likely to be extremely open and very sexual, relative to a girl who lives 15 minutes away.

Social circle text game

Realize that cold approach is a different ball game than Social Circle Game. If you are interested in picking up in your social circle (which is where you tend to pick up the hottest and most high quality women), there is no substitute to Social Circle Mastery .

In social circles, if you have followed Social Circle Mastery, you should be used to getting a woman's phone number after you are fairly certain that she is interested in you. Therefore, the numbers convert at a fairly high rate. At a minimum these women should reply to your texts, answer your phone calls, and most likely meet you for a date.

While social circle and cold approach Text and Phone Game are very similar, there are a few distinctions that make social circle text game markedly easier. The main difference is that if you take a woman's phone number in your social circle, you automatically enjoy a certain free level of comfort that is naturally built in to the situation. By merely meeting her through people she already trusts or taking her number after knowing each other for a period of time, you automatically have some level of comfort and commonality.

You also typically enjoy a higher level of investment early on with a girl from your social circle. This allows you to push the envelope with your attraction texts, reduces the time necessary before the first phone call and means that your efforts are more likely to lead to a date. Getting a girl to show up for a date through cold approach requires that you make very few mistakes, because the slightest disturbance in her attraction or comfort levels can lead to you losing her.

You can accidentally or tactically break many of the rules expounded in this book in your social circle. Because of the built in trust and comfort that is usually present, she will give you a 'free pass' for mistakes that would have spelled disaster in cold approach. However, following the rules in the book will only make your social circle numbers convert at an even higher rate.

CHAPTER 11 : Revitalizing Old Numbers

Chapter 11 - Revitalizing Old Numbers

Do not delete your old numbers. Oftentimes, men make the mistake of deleting old numbers because the woman did not reply after one text, stopped replying after a while, or any number of reasons communication ceased. Unless she flat out says, 'don't text/call me anymore', do not delete the number. Simply change your strategy and lower your expectations. This is a similar strategy to what you would do with a Long Fuse (previously discussed).

Women may come in and out of my life after weeks, months, and even years. Oftentimes, they get boyfriends and just cut communication off with all the other men in their life. When that relationship ends, a well timed text message will get you back in the game. This is why mastering the art of low compliance texting is so crucial.

This low compliance text strategy is applicable in a number of instances and is the foundation of what we call 'Slow Burn Game'. It does not matter how much time has passed (i.e. weeks, months, years). The key is that you make contact by Pinging.

How long should you wait before sending a recovery text? With numbers from cold approach, we want to allow some time, but not too much time, because they are more likely to forget who we are. As a general rule, wait a few days if you have texted more than twice in a row and have received no response.

What to text?

If you are not sure what to text, always default to light, non-needy call back humor. Below is a short list of possible text categories for what you can Ping a woman with when you have low compliance.

1. Non-needy humor in the form of a statement. For example:

    "After careful consideration, I have come to the conclusion that everyone in this Airport sucks except me. Tell your friends"

    "Nobu = best restaurant ever… just below Taco Bell. Why would anyone choose to use chop sticks? I would starve to death if that was all we had."

"Just dominated two 60 year old men at racket ball. Braddock's self esteem = All time high. :)"

"Just watched the movie 300. Turns out that movie is loosely based around my life. More specifically the character of Leonidus. :)"

"What do you call a fish with no eyes? A fsh. Buddum cha budum cha. I'll be here all week folks."

"It's not completely gay that we haven't hung out this week, but it's definitely pretty gay."

"Just wanted to let you know that the new and improved Braddock is 23% more awesome."

"Tequila 4. Braddock 0. I would kill a small child for a Tylenol."

"Mexican food place on Sunset and Le Brea = Better than sex."

2. Non-needy humor in the form of a short question. For example:

"Look up! Can you see the cloud that looks like a laughing koala from where you are?"

"Kim! If we don't hang out soon I'm breaking up with you for real this time. I'm changing my status on facebook and everything. :)"

"Heading to the gym... Need to build big muscles to overcompensate for small penis. Any other ideas?"

Braddock: *"Hey, can you help me out?"*
Girl: *"Help you with what?"*
Braddock: *"I want to meet up with this cute girl named [Girl's name], but she's impossible to nail down. Any advice? Keep in mind she's a total player."*

3. Inside jokes from the past. For example:

"Little Johnny called me and said he was lost. Some mother you are... if you lose him, I'm filing for divorce and I want everything."

"Make sure the kids have done their homework and dinner is on the

table. I've had a long day at work and don't need any more stress."

"See if your mother will watch the kids tonight. I think we need some alone time."

4. Intrigue texts that do not ask anything specific, but make her want to reply. For example:

    "The blue whale's tongue weighs more than an elephant. I saw it on the National Geographic channel."

    "I met someone who said they knew you today."

    "Guess what...."

    "You are not going to believe what happened to me today."

5. Pull heart strings. For example:

    "Just heard that Nelly song we used to always play....made me think of you :)

    "Just drove through B town... I figured the water tower would say "Home of Sara." :) Hope you are doing well."

    "X movie is on......made me think of you." [Note that this works better if there was a connection between the movie and the both of you]

Note that these usually need to be specific to the girl. These can get really deep if the memory was strong enough and the girl liked you a lot. However, they should be used sparingly. Using them more than a few times a YEAR will kill your chances with her.

6. Playing a funny false role and pretending that's why you guys have not talked. For example:

    "Did you join the peace corp or something?! I haven't seen you in forever.....I need some Kim in my life!"

    "Did you join The Marines or something? It's been ages! Come spoon me. That's an order."

"Us not talking for 2 months is going beyond playing hard to get. You're going to drive me into the arms of several other women at this rate."

7. Just jumping right into a wacky role play. For example:

"Hey, do me a favor and text me right back. Just hi or something. My friends don't believe retards can text. We'll show 'em lil buddy." (Source: TAF)

"Aliens are coming to abduct all the sexy people off the planet and force them to breed. You should be safe, I just wanted to text to say goodbye." (Source: TAF)

"Hi Kim!! Are we broken up for good? You don't, write, you never call, the kids are worried sick and rent was due 6 days ago!"

"We need to talk....I'm pretty sure I'm pregnant."

"You never write, you never call, rent's due and the kids are worried sick. What should I tell them?"

8. Mass texting something funny. For example:

"April 11, party at Movida. Kssshht, I repeat, the crisps are raiding the liquor store. Mother goose, over …"

"Hey all, Mike's farewell party at X bar Friday night. Your mission if you choose to accept it is to show up between the hours of 11pm and 2am. This message will self destruct in 30 sec! Hope to see you there…."

"Hey everyone, don't forget Kev's bday = our house tonight... swim suits = optional… arm floaties = required… safety first ;)"

"God I am awesome... that is all."

"Everyone sucks but me. Good talk."

"Just wanted to remind everyone that I'm cooler than the other side of the pillow. Tell your friends"

"Did you know that a blue whale's tongue weighs as much as an elephant?!? Gotta love Animal Planet"

Mass texting is a great way to reinitiate old numbers and to ping with a bunch of girls at the same time. Once you send out a mass text, if a girl responds, then you should start building value and using call back humor to build attraction again.

CHAPTER 12 : Flaking

Chapter 12 - Flaking

Flaking means canceling plans at the last minute, or not showing up. This will occasionally happen, especially on first dates.

To understand why flakes happen, let's look at an example of the thoughts of a typical attractive and social woman:

Kerry and Bill: An Illustrative Example of Why Flakes Happen

Kerry goes out to a restaurant with her friends. While waiting at the bar, an interesting man named Bill approaches her. About 3-5 minutes later (about how long it should take to get some attraction going), Bill asks for her number so they can "hang out sometime". At that moment, she genuinely would "hang out" with Bill "sometime".

In the moment when Bill asked for Kerry's phone number, Kerry decided to give it to him for a number of reasons:

- Bill was a great guy that Kerry could have been attracted too
- Kerry did not want to reject Bill and make things awkward
- Kerry was flattered by Bill's attention and wanted to show off in front of her friends

In truth, Kerry gave Bill her phone number for a combination of these reasons. Kerry did actually think that Bill had potential. The problem is that going out "sometime" is different from Kerry actually making plans to go out on say, a Thursday night.

Kerry is a desirable woman and as such, she rarely has "nothing else to do".

Thus, Bill has to represent an option that is more interesting and fun than anything else she could be doing including her friends, hobbies, work, other dates, or relaxing at home. That's a tough standard to meet. Kerry doesn't know just how tough it is and regularly complains that she never meets guys.

Over the next few days, Bill and Kerry exchange text messages. Bill subsequently calls Kerry and they set up a date. Kerry is nervous about the date because she does not really know Bill. Will Bill turn out to be boring?

Will the time they spend together be awkward? Will he just want to hook up with her even if things are not going well? Will she have to awkwardly reject him?

All of these things go through Kerry's mind on the day that she is supposed to meet Bill. Kerry experiences anxiety because of these thoughts. Two hours before Kerry is supposed to meet Bill, she gets a call from her good friend Kate, asking her if she wants to go and see a movie. Kerry has had a hard day at work and would love to see a movie. She has been unsure about meeting Bill the whole day. So she decides to accept Kate's offer. Kerry wants to tell Bill that she is no longer coming on their date but is nervous about his reaction. Moreover, she is now rushing to get ready for the movie. The chances are that she will delay sending Bill a text message to cancel the date until the last minute.

The end result? Bill did almost everything right. But Kerry flakes. And Bill waits.

Meeting up with a man that she barely knows is scary for most women. Of course, there is the obvious issue of physical safety. But more important in her mind is the issue that she may be forced to spend a number of uncomfortable and potentially socially awkward hours talking to a man that she may not like. To a man, the idea that you might not have a great time with this woman is not a big issue. The worst thing that can happen is you cut the date off early and go home. Men do not agonize and worry about whether the date will be socially awkward or not. But women do, and we as men need to take this into account.

Women also tend to be more analytical than men about social situations. She may wonder why you would even call her when you only met for a few minutes and you know so little about her. Are you desperate? Are you a player? Are you weird?

You can therefore see why a quick interaction leading to some basic attraction and "we should hang out sometime" is rarely going to inspire an exceptionally desirable woman into seeing you again. She fears safety, she fears social awkwardness and who are you anyway?

What should you do to avoid flakes?

Here are some more anti-flaking tactics for getting her phone number:

- Have something specific to do. Rather than simply say "let's hang out sometime", you can ask her to help you shop for your niece's birthday or something similar. Having an actual activity will make her look more forward to the date and give it some purpose.

- Bait her into suggesting the meet up. Let her chase you. Drop little hints ("I'm going to X" or "I'd love to do Y") and see if she tries to become part of those plans or says something like "That sounds fun; I'd love to do something like that". If she says this, take the chance to invite her out.

- Do not make the date, or the phone number exchange, the last part of your interaction. Doing this can make the interaction feel like a pickup as opposed to a genuine interaction. Consequently, stay at least 5 minutes after the interaction and continue talking to her and flirting in this 5 minutes if possible.

- Engage her friends. When she goes home, her friends should be excited that she met you. To a woman, her friends' approval for the men she dates is very important.

- Focus on the date, not the phone number. The phone should be an afterthought (and it is not always strictly necessary, although you take a big risk that she will not think your plans are serious if you do not get her number).

- Set up callback humor. If you can create a running joke during your interaction or have a nickname for her, you can use this when you phone her later on as funny material. Using these jokes or nicknames can often trigger a reversal to the emotional state that she was in when she first met you. She will be brought back to the world of being out, having fun and meeting men as opposed to whatever mundane thing she was actually doing when you called.

- Program your number into her phone. Many people will not answer the phone if they do not know who is calling. If you program your number into her phone, she will know that it is you. Ideally, you would set up even more callback humor by programming your name as "My hero" or "Mr. T" or anything else that is playfully relevant to the situation.

- If she is strongly interested in you at the first inter action and you both connect well, tell her exactly when you will call and get her to promise to answer. However, do not make this sound too serious.

What should you do if a woman flakes?

Here is the best thing to do when a woman who you are not currently dating flakes:

Nothing!

Do not be upset. Do not lecture her. The truth is that she probably does not care that she missed the date because if she cared enough, she probably would not have flaked in the first place. Ask yourself, 'would she have flaked if the date was with Brad Pitt?'

> **A Tough Reality**
>
> Let's say you planned to meet her at 6pm. You had to leave work early. You had to drive like mad and fight traffic. You had to cut your workout short. You had to miss your favorite show. But you are here and on time for your date.
>
> And she doesn't show up.
>
> Tough luck. She doesn't care. That is not her problem. You should not have committed so much for a woman that you hardly know. If you tell her all of this, you have just lost value in her eyes because you rearranged your life for a date with her. If you really want this woman, keep it to yourself and be unreactive.

The answer is 'no'. The reason is simply because you did not have the requisite value to get her to want to come on a date with you.

Any 'punishing' that you do will simply make her associate you with bad emotions and make her feel bad momentarily (but will soon be forgotten and will not help your chances). Instead, remember the principle of 'preselection' and act like a man who has plenty of women interested in him. Such a man would not be especially thrown off by the flake. He has other women in his life who would love see him, and more likely than not, whatever it was that he was going to do with her was something that he would enjoy doing anyway with cool friends. If this frame is not perfectly clear and obvious to you, you can even try to cancel the next time you set up a date with a random woman. Listen for her reaction and learn to copy it. You will see that it did not ruin her day and that it should not ruin yours.

A phrase that you can use if she cancels is, "no problem, I'll invite someone else". This is best used when your plans were obviously for two people (for example, you had two concert tickets and invited her). Do not use this on a third or fourth date, but rather while the relationship is still casual.

Closing Remarks

We hope that you have enjoyed this book and have gotten a lot out of it.

Make sure you read and review this book on a regular basis. Use it as a reference guide and a resource which you can refer back to again and again.

It is now up to you to apply the techniques you have learned. While the book has given you the key techniques, strategies, mindsets and tactics, the only way that you will get good at Text and Phone Game is by going out there and doing it! *Remember - the best way to get good is by getting good information and using it immediately yourself.*

You have in front of you the tools to be extremely good at Text and Phone Game. However, a great skill never came to anyone without practice, so the closing advice from both of us (Braddock and Mr M) is to get out in the field and do it.

We really hope you have enjoyed this book. We've put a lot of hard work into it, and we'd really appreciate it if you dropped us a line to let us know what you think. Our email addresses are:

braddock@lovesystems.com and mrm@lovesystems.com.

Warm regards,

Braddock and Mr M

Further Education

When you're ready to take your skills to the next level, be sure to check out other Love Systems products, workshops and specialty seminars, including SOCIAL CIRCLE MASTERY and the INNER GAME SEMINAR, two special courses designed by Mr M and Braddock.

Magic Bullets is the bible of dating and seduction. Written by Nick Savoy, Magic Bullets explains the complete system for meeting and dating beautiful women. If you are completely new to Love Systems or you want to improve your game, it is highly recommended to get yourself a copy of Magic Bullets. Everything of Love Systems is based on this book.

The Routines Manual is one of the most popular books in dating and seduction. Senior Love Systems The Don wrote the book with the help of Nick Savoy. There are two different copies available. The first Routines Manual is a comprehensive guide to learning and mastering use of routines. It not only explains how and why routines work, but also provides a compilation of hundreds of the very best and most effective routines used by the world's best dating coaches. The second edition has even more secret routines for day game, touching, seduction, and more.

The Relationship Management DVD series teaches you how to have a good relationships with your partner and keeping it successful. It answers the question, what do you do after you get the girl? Whether you want to have a casual relationship, monogamy, multiple relationships or threesomes, Nick Savoy goes in depth how to manage your relationship.

Love Systems also provides live training in forms of workshops (bootcamps). Over a course of three days with seminars (15 hours) and infield training (8 hours) you will learn from the best dating coaches how to succeed with women. It is the fastest way to learn how to meet and date beautiful women.

SOCIAL CIRCLE MASTERY has been heralded by past students as 're-volutionary', 'the next step in game' and 'integral to building a life'. It reveals the groundbreaking systems, social theories and social techniques that can allow an ordinary person to live a life filled with 10s (ultra-beautiful women) and get girls with uncanny consistency - not from cold approach, but through building an enviable social circle and social life. SOCIAL CIRCLE MASTERY also covers the revolutionary structure/

model/process of seducing women that you meet through social events, such as dinner parties, work events, house parties, hobby classes or even random introductions. You may have thought the guys who all the girls in your social circles were attracted to were just 'charismatic' or 'outgoing'. Wrong. It is a completely learnable trait, skill and system. Learning how to fill your social circle with beautiful women and to be the alpha male within that group is at the heart of the SOCIAL CIRCLE MASTERY seminar. See the reviews here.

The powerful INNER GAME SEMINAR is the most ground breaking advancement in dating science. It is designed to get you to achieve the highest level of ability with women. The seminar aims at creating TRUE NATURALS with women and facilitates POWERFUL INNER GAME CHANGE that will skyrocket your ability with HOT WOMEN (and we're talking the true 9s and 10s here). Students have been left RAVING about their LIFE CHANGING experience at the INNER GAME SEMINAR. See the reviews here.

FREE Resources to Improve Your Game

Links to Articles by Mr M

Why Inner Game Is The Most Important Part Of TRUE Success With Women
The Comprehensive Guide To Attraction
Never before revealed Nordic and European techniques - Pick up and Female Psychology
ACHIEVING SOCIAL DOMONANCE: How To Become The Alpha Male In Social Situations
The Basis of Natural Game - The Inverted Seduction Principle
INNER GAME - the Secret of Attractive Reactiveness
Guide To Qualification
Revealing the Social Matrix Part 1: The Structure of your Social Life
Revealing the Social Matrix Part 2: The Hidden Structure to Social Circle Pick Ups

Links to Articles by Braddock

Oneitus??
Q and A on Love
Braddock`s Inner Game
Change your life NOW!!!!!!!!
Q and A : Approach Anexiety
„I don`t chase......I replace."
Do you bring value or take it?????
Text Game By Braddock
Text Game Basics by Braddock and Savoy
Braddock`s prescription to move out of the LJBF Zone
Spring Break Game: Braddock`s Definitive Guide (Guaranteed to get you laid)
Social Circle vs. Cold Approach ... Let`s just hug it out

Terms and Conditions

Limit of Liability/Disclaimer of Warranty: The publisher and the author make no representation of warranties with respect to the accuracy or completeness of the contents of this work and specifically disclaim all warranties, including without limitation, warranties of fitness for a particular purpose. No warranty may be created or extended by sales or promotional materials. The advice and strategies contained herein may not be suitable for every situation. This work is provided with the understanding that the publisher is not engaged in rendering legal, accounting, or other professional services. If professional assistance is required, the services of a competent professional person should be sought. Neither the publisher nor the author shall be liable for damages arising here from. The fact that an organization or Website is referred to in this work as a citation and/or a potential source of further information does not mean that the author or publisher endorses the information the organization or Website may provide or recommendations it may make. Further, readers should be aware that Internet Websites listed in this work may have changed or disappeared between when this work was written and when it is read.

All product names, logos and artwork are copyrights of their respective owners. None of the owners have sponsored or endorsed this publication. Images used within this publication content and are licensed and purchased through istockphoto, photos, stockxpert, and fotalia. com. While all attempts have been made to verify information provided, the author assumes no responsibility for errors, omissions, or contrary interpretation on the subject matter herein. Any perceived slights of peoples or organizations are unintentional. The purchaser or reader of this publication assumes responsibility for the use of these materials and information. No guarantees of income are made. The author reserves the right to make changes and assumes no responsibility or liability whatsoever on behalf of any purchaser or reader of these materials.

Contributors To This Book

Nick (Savoy) – (Los Angeles, CA) is President and CEO of Love Systems and is the author of Magic Bullets, our 'bible' of dating science and social dynamics. Savoy is also the co creator of **The Routines Manual Volume I** and **The Routines Manual Volume II** and the cutting edge **Relationship Management DVD series**. Check out **Savoy's Blog.**

Braddock – (Los Angeles, CA) is a Love Systems lead instructor. Besides teaching bootcamps, Braddock is also co creator of the following Love Systems seminars: **Inner Game, Social Circle Mastery,** and **Strippers and Hired Guns**. TSB Magazine recently ranked Braddock the "Number 4 Pickup Artist in the World." Check out **Braddock's Blog.**

Mr. M – (London, England) is a Love Systems senior instructor. Besides teaching live bootcamps, Mr. M is also the director of Love Systems Europe. Besides co writing and editing this book, Mr. M is also co creator of the **Inner Game** and **Social Circle Mastery** seminars.

Daxx – (Los Angeles, CA) is a junior instructor for Love Systems. Daxx is a rising star with Love Systems and one of our youngest instructors. He recently moved from London to Los Angeles. Check out **Daxx's Blog.**

Big Business – (New York City, NY) is a junior instructor for Love Systems and is the creator of the Humor, Improv, and Attraction seminar. Besides doing the humor seminar, Big Business is available for 1 on 1's as well. Check out **Big Business's Blog**.

Dubbsy – (Los Angeles, CA) is a junior instructor for Love Systems. He is one of the newest members of the Love Systems team. Along with Daxx, he is also one of the youngest members of the team. Dubbsy is working on a College Game seminar with Braddock. Check out **Dubbsy's Blog.**

Congratulations on investing in *The Ultimate Guide to Text and Phone Game* by Braddock and Mr. M! To download your exclusive bonus chapter (Situations & Scenarios), click here:

www.LoveSystems.com/ultimateguidebonusdownload

www.ingramcontent.com/pod-product-compliance
Lightning Source LLC
Chambersburg PA
CBHW072127290426
44111CB00012B/1815